AUTHOR IMPRESSIONS

"Over the last decade or so that I've known Dr. Coyte Cooper he has impressed me with his diligence, intelligence, and values. He is an effective teacher, an engaged mentor, a cutting edge scholar, and, most importantly to me, a caring and dedicated husband, father, and friend. From his impressive background in sports participation to his impressive scholarly resume as a sport researcher today, Dr. Cooper is a leader who provides insights by which we all can benefit."

—Paul M. Pedersen, PhD, Professor & Director, Sport Management
(Indiana University)

"Having the opportunity to get to know Dr. Cooper has had a tremendous impact on my overall personal and professional growth. He truly understands the importance of building positive relationships that make lasting impressions. He lives each and every day with gratitude, energy, and a sincere excitement for helping others around him, and I've become better in all aspects of my life because of his impact."

—Scott Grant, Instructor, College of Business (The University of Findlay)

"It has been said that 'our reputation is what people think of us, but our character is who we are.' In Impressions, Coyte helps us understand the relationship between our brand and our character. This is an outstanding book for all readers as it is an excellent reminder for experienced leaders and provides wonderful insights to young people developing their networks and careers."

—Bubba Cunningham, Director of Athletics (University of North Carolina)

"Very few people have impacted my life the way Coyte Cooper has. I'm constantly looking to Coyte for both inspiration and sharp ideas on business, branding, and life in general. Trust me, the amount of knowledge this guy has and the level of success he's achieved in sports, entrepreneurship, and in his personal relationships is unparalleled. I only know one person on the planet who is an NCAA Division I All-American athlete, a Ph.D. professor, and an amazing husband and father. His name is Coyte Cooper. The bottom line is Coyte understands what's important in life and he understands people."

—Isaiah Hankel, Ph.D., Author of Black Hole Focus

"Passion, energy, and dedication are three words that individuals often use after a first, second, or decade worth of impressions working with Coyte Cooper. He is the embodiment of the powerful words of wisdom encapsulated within these pages and I am grateful I've had the opportunity to learn from and work with him throughout my career."

—Erianne Weight, Ph.D., Assistant Professor & Undergraduate Coordinator
(University of North Carolina Sport Administration)

"Dr. Coyte Cooper is among the most respected and admired professionals in the sport management industry. He has earned this position of prestige not due to selfish ambition and neglecting relationships, but rather a relentless commitment to selflessly add value to those people around him. Through Dr. Cooper's leadership I have been challenged to refine my personal brand and position myself to pursue excellence while embracing my core values. I am proud of the professional goals I have accomplished in large part due to Dr. Cooper's mentorship, but I am most honored and humbled that impressions he has made on my life translate to my personal relationships and family pursuits as well!"

—Landon Huffman, Ph.D., Assistant Professor of Sport Studies, Guilford College

IMPRESSIONS

The Power of Personal Branding in Living an Extraordinary Life

IMPRESSIONS

THE POWER OF PERSONAL
BRANDING IN LIVING
AN EXTRAORDINARY LIFE

COYTE G. COOPER, PH.D.

IMPRESSIONS:
The Power of Personal Branding in Living an Extraordinary Life

Copyright © 2014 Coyte G. Cooper, Ph.D.

Cover design by Cliff Fretwell
Interior design by Ted Ruybal
Manufactured in the United States of America

For more information, please contact:

Wisdom House Books
www.wisdomhousebooks.com
www.coytecooper.com

Paperback:
ISBN 13: 978-0-9905636-0-0
ISBN 10: 0-9905636-0-X
LCCN: 2014912552
SEL027000 SELF-HELP / Personal Growth / Success
1 2 3 4 5 6 7 8 9 10

Dedicated to my beautiful wife Brandy, who has supported me throughout this process and has provided me with unconditional love.

And to my little ones Carter and Mya, for inspiring me daily to want to be a better person.

CONTENTS

ACKNOWLEDGMENTS

This book would not have been possible without all of the amazing people who have made an impression on my life throughout the years. There is no one that has influenced how I approach my life on a daily basis more than my parents, Gene and Lisa. Thank you so much for putting me first and for teaching me how to live the right way. I would also like to thank my brother Matt for always being a true friend and for listening to my ideas throughout this process.

Another person who made this book possible is my wife, Brandy, who has always supported me and encouraged me to chase my dreams. In addition, she did an amazing job putting the final editing touches on the book with her fine attention to detail. Thanks so much for your help and for allowing me to pursue this passion!

I would also like to show my gratitude to the mentors throughout the years who have left a lasting impression on my life. In particular, thanks to Ron Bessemer and Paul Pedersen for being selfless mentors who showed me how to live through modeling.

Another group I would like to thank is the colleagues who have supported me throughout the years. In particular, in addition to all of my current UNC colleagues, thanks to my good friends Erianne Weight, Jason Mihalik, and Landon Huffman for encouraging me while writing this book. I would also like to extend my appreciation for all of the amazing people who wrote testimonials to be included in the book.

There are some people I would like to thank for helping put the book together in the final stages. Cliff Fretwell did an amazing job with the concept and graphics for the book cover and I am grateful for that. Ted Ruybal went above and beyond expectations when designing the interior for the book and was a pleasure to work with throughout the process. I would also like to thank Arielle Hebert and Wisdom House Books for helping to edit the book. Finally, I would like to express my gratitude to my Elite Level Sport Marketing (ELSM) interns Blake Moushon, Chris Jaques, Joe Smaldone, Madison Miller, Michael Diaz, and Susan Wallrich for helping to promote the book so that it gets in the hands of people.

Thank you to all of my clients who have allowed me to work with their companies, organizations, teams, and individuals. It is these opportunities that have allowed me to fully understand how impressions can impact people's lives.

One final thanks to the individuals who take the time to read this book! It is my hope that it will add value to your life so that you can make the types of impressions on people that will change the world!

FOREWORD

"To each there comes in their lifetime a special moment when they are figuratively tapped on the shoulder and offered the chance to do a very special thing, unique to them and fitted to their talents. What a tragedy if that moment finds them unprepared or unqualified for that which could have been their finest hour."

—*Winston Churchill*

I f you are reading this book, then you are looking for a way to gain some kind of edge in your life. My hope is that you are searching for strategies to enhance the quality of your living so that you can make extraordinary impressions on the people around you. If so, then this is the book for you because it will focus on exactly what it means to establish a brand vision for yourself and then it will outline the steps necessary to make it a reality. You see, the truth is that personal branding is nothing more than determining exactly what type of person you would like to become someday and then being proactive about making it a reality. Of course, branding also has to do with the perceptions that other people have of you based on your interactions with them. The good news for you is that you simply need to become a person that adds tremendous value to the people around you. When you are able to do this, then you will develop an extraordinary personal brand that will open up opportunities to you in all areas of your life. However, you need to be ready to make sacrifices because developing an extraordinary brand takes an extraordinary approach to life. It will require a mindset in which you are ready to get up and embrace each day with a proactive mindset.

This book is broken down into 14 different chapters that are designed to give you an understanding of personal brand and the steps that are necessary to realize your full potential. In the Early Planning phase (chapters #1-4), the focus is on the foundational elements necessary to understand the concept of personal branding and developing a brand vision that will guide your efforts moving forward. These are key areas that will cultivate energy in your life, as you will be taking the time necessary to really know the things that you are truly passionate about. After this, the middle Implementation phase of the book (chapters #5-10) will emphasize the concepts and steps that are necessary to make your vision a reality through the daily decisions you make. The final Follow Through phase (chapters #11-14) will build on the Implementation phase by providing additional insights that are critical for personal branding initiatives.

THE VISION FOR THE BOOK

The overall goal for this book is very simple: I want to add value to your life by helping you to understand some basic action steps that you can take to improve relationships and to increase the opportunities available to you in your life. If I were able to accomplish this with just one person, then all the hard work that was put into this book would truly be worthwhile. I hope that reading this book will both inform and inspire you to realize your full potential so that you are able to live an extraordinary life. As you move through the book, you will quickly realize that you must learn to see things from other people's perspectives if you are going to achieve success in your life. The awesome thing about personal branding is how empowering it is when you start to grasp the concept and realize the control you have over the perceptions that people have of you. It is completely within your reach to control the way that you approach each interaction that you have with people on a daily basis. When you gain a full understanding of the potential that this small decision presents, the sky is the limit on what you will be able to achieve in your life.

CHANGE STARTS TODAY

The first thing that I need you to understand is that you have the ability to change your life today. The initial motion is very simple in that you need to decide whether or not you are interested in making adjustments to realize your full potential. Once this decision has been made, you simply need to read through each of the chapters and apply the different concepts to your life. While change can happen instantaneously, you must understand that the perceptions that people have of you may take longer to change, depending on the decisions that you have made in the past. However, if you are consistent with your efforts over extended periods of time (e.g., 2-3 months), you will eventually see the quality of your relationships drastically improve. Once you get to the point where you are adding value to others on a regular basis, you will be on track to have a unique personal brand and opportunities will open up that you never previously thought possible.

TIME TO GET TO WORK

If you are still reading, then you are likely ready to take steps to develop a personal brand that will enhance the quality in all areas of your life. If not, then it is still pretty early in the book and there is still a strong chance that something will click that will inspire you to take action. Now that we have a basic understanding of the purpose of the book, it is time to get to work! As you read through each chapter, take the time to make sure that you are fully implementing the concepts successfully into your life. And once you are done reading the chapter, be sure to answer the "Chapter Exercises," as they will help you to apply the concepts being learned. Finally, when you move through the book, chase your passion so that you instill an energy into your life that will drive you to reach your full potential. By the time you reach the end of the book, it is my hope that you will be a completely different person than when you started! It is time for you to learn how to live an extraordinary life!

PHASE 1

Foundational Elements
to Extraordinary Branding

Early Planning

CHAPTER 1

What The Heck is Personal Branding, and Why Does it Matter?

"Your brand is what people say about you when you are not in the room."

—*Jeff Bezos, Founder of Amazon*

Whenever I talk to audiences about personal branding, I am clear about the fact that it IS NOT a quick strategy to impress people in an inauthentic manner. While it is sometimes portrayed this way, it is about far more than making quick fixes to impress people quickly so you can advance your career. The reality is that the easy route is rarely the one that brings meaningful, lasting results that will improve your life. This comes from a commitment to living the right way so that you will make positive impressions on the people around you on a consistent basis. This is exactly what personal branding is about and this will be the central focus of the book. The goal is to help you make decisions that will enhance your life in all areas that are important to you. The good news is that the fundamental concepts in personal branding can help you to make decisions that will maximize your potential in each of these areas.

WHAT EXACTLY IS PERSONAL BRANDING?

When I discuss personal branding with people, I am quick to point out that it has nothing to do with talking in third person and giving yourself new names, like you see with some select professional athletes. It is also not about doing things that get you attention for the wrong reasons. Personal branding is about building a reputation with the people around you that will allow you to cultivate and enhance relationships that open up opportunities in your life. For some people, branding will be about enhancing their overall quality of life because the concepts allow them to be more cognizant of the things that matter most to the important people in their life. Thus, the branding process allows us to add meaningful value to other people's lives, which often results in adding value to our own lives.

When broken down to the simplest explanation, personal branding is a concept that is both easy to comprehend and highly impactful. It starts with the concept of understanding that the people around you all have perceptions about the type of person you are. They may not consciously think about this, but everyone intuitively assesses the interactions going on around them and it eventually results in their making instinctual judgments about people. This is where personal branding comes into play. These intuitive assessments that people make eventually add up and they become a part of what people think about us. When these interactions are consistently positive because you are living the right way, then people's perceptions of you are likely to be positive as well. Personal branding is simply an extension of this concept as it encompasses the things people think when they come in to contact with you in some manner. The goal of this book is to get you to embrace personal branding so that you can make decisions that will ensure that these perceptions are positive. Given that relationships are so important to success in life, it is essential that you learn to cultivate a positive brand that will open up new opportunities that enhance your life.

BRANDING IS A LIFESTYLE

When you gain an understanding of personal branding, it is easy to grasp the fact that it is a lifestyle that you commit to living every single day. Because it is directly influenced by the individual daily interactions you have with people, you need to teach yourself to be great at making sound decisions on a consistent basis. When they are guided by sound values (discussed in Chapter 4), you have the opportunity to realize a vision (Chapter 3) that will truly enhance your life and allow you to realize your full potential. But it is important to understand that there is nothing quick about the process of personal branding. Then again, what worthwhile achievements in life are realized without a real significant commitment? If you hope to realize a personal brand that is associated with special accomplishments, then you need to be ready to commit to an extraordinary lifestyle. Living your values daily needs to simply be a part of who you are as a person, and you MUST be stubborn and persistent about making it happen. There should be so much passion about realizing your vision that you will absolutely get back on track when you encounter challenges. When it becomes a lifestyle, you will eventually build a personal brand that is worthy of your full potential.

THE COMMONALITY BETWEEN BRANDING AND LEADERSHIP

Leadership is all about making decisions that will influence the people around us in a positive way. When you learn to add value to these individuals, you will build credibility with them and they will be more likely to follow you in your pursuit to realize your vision. With this description, you can see where personal branding really has a lot in common with leadership. As we will discuss later in the book, much of the success in both of these areas has to do with your ability to consider other people's interests/needs, and then making decisions that will build your reputation with them. However, the ability to accomplish these things is largely dependent on your capability to lead yourself in modeling the values that are most important to you. It is extremely difficult to build positive relationships with people and cultivate a strong personal brand when you cannot get yourself to live the way you know you should be living.

IT'S ABOUT LEARNING TO LEAD YOURSELF

One of the most important elements of personal branding is learning to live the values that are most important to you on a daily basis. Your values are the attributes for which you hope to become known over time (e.g., integrity, kindness, passion) and it takes a constant awareness of your actions surrounding these values to realize your brand vision. Once you know exactly who you would like to become, it is about taking the time to know how to get there and then simply having the self-discipline to do the little things on a consistent basis. However, it is important to note that follow through is often the most difficult element of personal branding because it takes a strong focus to pursue your vision when things are not going smoothly. One of the first steps to making this happen is being committed to becoming a master of leading yourself. What this means is that you must teach yourself to model your values during individual interactions with people. If you want to be known as an extremely positive person, then you need to be proactive about waking up each morning with energy for the day. One way to make sure you get off to a solid start is by spending the first five minutes focusing on the things you are most grateful for in your life. Being a master of leading yourself means you must be able to follow through on initiatives like this every single day so it can become a part of who you are. The goal is for you to have a set structure with initiatives just like this, so by the end of this book you are ready to do what is necessary to live an extraordinary life.

THE DIFFERENCE BETWEEN IDEAS AND IMPLEMENTATION

As you read through this book, it is my hope that you will start to form ideas about the type of person you would like to become in the future. That is an extremely important step in personal branding because you must have a vision that you plan to pursue daily. This will help cultivate a passion that will energize you as you get started on your pursuit to realize your full potential. With that being said, your ideas will be nothing if you are not able to implement them successfully both immediately and in the long run. As you move through this book, it will be essential that you develop the ability to take instant steps to model your values. While the identification of knowing you want to be recognized as a creative person is great, it will result in nothing if you do not seek out innovative initiatives to develop your skill sets. You will need to become a person of consistent action to make this happen. Pride yourself on being a person that follows through on your intentions and you will always be a step closer to realizing your peak personal brand.

WHY DOES IT EVEN MATTER?

You may be asking yourself, "Why does it even matter what perceptions people have of me?" or, "I can't please everyone so why even bother?" There is certainly some value in asking these questions. The truth is that there are times when you should not dwell on worrying about what other people think about you. There are some people that you will not be able to influence regardless of your actions and/or intentions. As explained by the great essayist, lecturer, and poet Ralph Waldo Emerson, "Whatever course you decide on, there will always be someone to tell you that you are wrong." The important thing here is not to dwell on this because there a large number of people that you will be able to make a positive impression on if you have the right mindset and approach. With these people, you have the opportunity to shape the way that they will think about you if you are willing to follow through on the concepts in this book. And why does this matter? Well, I'll tell you why. Nearly all aspects of life where you hope to be "successful" are directly influenced by your ability to build solid relationships. If you are a college student and want to position yourself to get a job, then you need to build your brand with your professors and internship coordinators so they will speak extremely well on your behalf. If you are hoping to get a promotion in your current job, then you better identify the areas that are important to the higher ups and make it a priority in your life. And if you are passionate about building a better relationship with your partner, it would make sense that you consider his or her needs and make an effort to add value to their life. All of these things have to do with your ability to enhance the perceptions that key individuals in your life have of you. These things are all influenced by your ability to develop a solid personal brand. The goal is to teach you to combine all the important areas in your life so you can develop a brand vision that you can pursue on a daily basis.

TAKE HOME POINT— BRANDING IS A DAILY LIFESTYLE

Personal branding is a concept that has the potential to change your life in extraordinary ways, but it takes a major commitment on your part to make it a reality. The success of nearly all important endeavors that are worth pursuing in life are highly dependent on your ability to build relationships, and personal branding ensures that you are taking steps to make a positive impression on others. The first thing that you must recognize is that it will require a lifestyle in which you commit to living the values that are most important to you. Once you have identified these values, it is time for you to become a master of implementation and modeling in your every day living. It will not always be easy to follow through on your intentions, but it is certainly possible if you commit fully to building an extraordinary brand that allows you to reach your full potential in all areas of your life. If you are able to take these steps, then you will cultivate strong relationships that will open up unique opportunities in your life. And most importantly, you will be living the life that you truly want to live, bringing happiness to your life. Now that we understand what it will take, it is time to get to work on developing an extraordinary life and personal brand!

IMPRESSIONS IMPLEMENTATION EXERCISE

As we get started, it is important to start thinking of the current personal brand that you have with people in your life. Because personal brand has a lot to do with other people's perceptions of you, it is essential to reflect on how your actions have impacted the important people in your life. Answer the questions below before moving on to the next chapter.

1. Think about the way that you interact with people on a daily basis. If you are being honest with yourself, are there times where you are the cause of negative interactions with people? We all have these moments, so don't be afraid to own them here. Write the main negative interactions down and move to the next question.

2. What impacts do these negative interactions have on the perceptions that people (both this person and others) have of you? Determine now if this is something that is worth changing because it is influencing your brand with others.

3. What steps could you take to turn this into a positive interaction so that you are able to build stronger relationships with others? What are the implications if you make this happen?

CHAPTER 2

You Already Have a Brand . . .
You Probably Just Don't Know It

"Personal branding is about managing your name—even if you don't own a business—in a world of misinformation, disinformation, and semi-permanent Google records. Going on a date? Chances are that your "blind" date has Googled your name. Going to a job interview? Ditto."

—Tim Ferriss, Author of the 4-Hour Work Week

Everybody has a brand. In fact, all people have multiple brands depending on whom they interact with, but few people know this because they have never spent the time to think about how their actions influence other people's perceptions of them. For most people, they move from one day to the next with little thought as to how their daily decisions influence their personal brand. And what these individuals do not realize is that this comes at a significant cost because it limits their ability to reach their full potential. The simple reality is that you cannot maximize the positive opportunities in life if you are not considering how you are interacting with others on a regular basis. The good news is that you can turn this around in an instant if you are willing to spend the time to understand personal branding and the strategies you need to embrace to make sound decisions on a daily basis.

BRANDING HAS BROAD-REACHING IMPLICATIONS

When most people think about branding, they immediately think of individuals in business that are looking for ways to differentiate themselves so they can advance their careers. And while it certainly encompasses this particular situation, personal branding can also extend to any area of your life if you are willing to spend the time to apply the concepts to the different roles you fill on a daily basis (e.g., boss, coach, employee, parent, teacher). When you consider the fact that branding involves the thoughts that come to mind when others come in to contact with you, then you quickly realize that this is something that directly relates to each of the key relationships that you have in your life. To ensure that this hits home, we will touch on some of the key situations in which these branding concepts come into play in this chapter. Once you see these, I think you will grasp the fact that personal branding is a philosophy that you need to embrace immediately and effectively in your life. If you do, there is no doubt that you will see the quality of your life improve drastically because you will be making decisions to build your relationships with people.

BRANDING IS A DAILY CONSIDERATION

The interesting thing is that most people seem to think that personal branding only applies to professional environments. This could not be further from the truth. When it comes to our lives, we already have a brand with every single person whom we consider to be important to us. We also have a brand with people whom we consider "less important," but we may not care nearly as much about the implications here (more on the importance of changing this mindset later, because every impression does matter). While people do not consciously think about what your brand is, they intuitively draw conclusions about the type of person that you are based on your actions when you are around them. When these are consistently positive over time, then they will draw positive conclusions about you and this will result in a certain level of preferred status with them. On the flip side, when you are constantly making poor decisions that negatively influence the people around you, then they will likely have a negative perception of you that will cause them to distance themselves from you in the future. Do this often enough and you will not have many people around you, let alone to help enhance your life.

BRANDING'S INFLUENCE ON NORMAL LIVING

So, you may already be considering whether or not personal branding influences your life at all. Let me ask you this: have you ever had somebody that was truly special to you because of what they added to your life? My hope is that all of you answer yes to this question. For the individuals whom this rings true, I would like you to take a moment to think about all of the reasons why you appreciated this individual. In other words, what did they do on a regular basis to influence your life? Take a moment to do this right now before moving forward.

⤮

I am going to go out on a limb and say that everything that you listed likely related to the care that they had for you as a person. I would like you to do something else now. Based on these answers, how would you describe this person to someone if you were asked? Take a moment to do this before reading on.

⤮

So, why did I ask you to do this exercise? Well, the reason is actually quite simple when you think about it. This demonstrates the concept of personal branding that takes place in our daily lives on a regular basis. We are constantly interacting with others literally hundreds to thousands of times daily through personal and electronic interactions, and we are making impressions without even knowing it. And often, if we are not paying attention to how these interactions influence other people's perceptions (our brand), then we are neglecting opportunities to build stronger relationships in our lives. The point here is that our interactions always matter with people, and when we take control of them with a vision in mind, we have an opportunity to make a positive impression on a wide range of people.

There is another point that I would like to make regarding the exercise. I asked you to do the exercise about somebody influential in your life for a couple of reasons. First, it is assumed that most people can relate to this example because nearly everyone has at least one person who has positively impacted their lives. Second, the situation accurately demonstrates the influence of positive interactions because we are discussing an individual who made decisions that made an impression on us. We could have easily done the opposite and focused on someone who has hurt us, but it makes more sense to focus on positive influences because it will help you better distinguish people in your life who have affected you with their interactions and personal brand. Finally, this situation demonstrates the benefits of positive personal branding. The person you wrote about is someone who did things the right way and built a strong relationship with you that left a lasting impression. As a result, it is my guess that you would have gone out of your way to help them if they ever needed it. While this should never be a priority, it is certainly a benefit of taking control of interactions and personal brand on a daily basis. Now consider the implications if you made a habit of doing this regularly with as many people as possible. By taking control of your interactions in a positive, pro-active manner, you can build outstanding relationships that will add value to your life. In the process, you will become known as a person who is truly worth being around because you will know how to add value to others. If this is not something that makes sense yet, I believe that it will by the end of the book, so read on.

ROLE PLAYING IN PERSONAL BRANDING

It is important that we establish the specific roles that are influenced by personal branding early in the book. The standard response would be that the concepts influence any role that you have in your life that includes relationships and interactions with others. Authentic branding is a universal approach in which we live in a certain way regardless of whom we interact with. However, at this point in the book, this lack of specificity may not inspire action because it can be both overwhelming and/or unclear. The reality is that this personal branding concept must hit close to home for you to truly buy-in and make it a part of your daily living. So, we are going to visit some examples below that will illustrate the ways that branding can influence key areas of our life.

Example 1: The Role of Parent

If you are a parent, you have interactions every single day that make an impression on your kid(s). All of these individual actions count towards the type of person that your child will become. When you are consistently supportive and are striving to add value to their lives daily, then you give your children the best chance to succeed in their future. And, in the times that you are calm, loving, and encouraging, you teach them what it is like to be these things through modeling. This could be any number of attributes, but you get the point. In addition to the impact that you have on your kids, you are also building a brand with your children. And while kids don't usually reflect on this until later in life, you can be sure that the interactions are intuitively being collected and that someday they will be able to assess the type of parent that you are/were. Hopefully, you are making the types of decisions that will allow your kids to say that you were an amazing parent who always put them first and showed them how to live life the right way. In the meantime, understand that all of your daily decisions matter. When you are impatient with your kids on a regular basis, then you will eventually be seen as an impatient parent to them. And when you tell them to do something, but do the exact opposite, then they may eventually see you as a hypocrite. If it matters to you, think hard about what you would like your kids to think about you someday and make sure your daily actions are in alignment with this vision.

Example 2: The Role of Partner/Spouse

One of the biggest mistakes that partners make in a relationship is that they fail to see things from the other person's perspective. They approach each interaction assessing things from their own perspective and never consider the fact that the other people may be seeing things another way. The reality is that we all have different backgrounds that have influenced the way that we experience the world. So, you are probably asking yourself what this even means. Well, let me tell you. You have likely made decisions at some point in your life for which your partner has seen you as inconsiderate and you did not even realize it. Personally, when first applying personal branding concepts, I quickly became aware of instances in which I had regularly failed to consider how my actions were influencing my wife. And as a result, I made decisions that were based on my preferences and likely created strains in the relationship that could have easily been avoided. If you truly care about someone, you will stop and take the time to think about the things that they value most, so you can ensure that you are building a strong relationship with him/her. If you want a person to think of you as a caring, supportive partner, then you need to make sure that your actions model this based on his/her expectations. The follow through on this act will ensure that you are building a positive brand with your partner.

Example 3: The Role of Co-Worker

Everyone has likely had co-workers, classmates, and/or colleagues that have behaved in an inappropriate manner in the workplace. Whether they were overbearing, opinionated, and/or over zealous, they often had a negative impact on the work environment because they were unpleasant to work with. As a result, if someone asked about them, you could quickly tell them your opinion because they made a strong, negative impression on you. Based on your understanding already, you know that this was your perception based on interactions. And if this was consistent with others, this is likely what their personal brand was in the office. It is probably easy for you to describe the influence that this had on the person's ability to develop relationships with others in your workplace. Now that we have made this point, consider how your actions influence others in your place of business. Is your personal brand with co-workers positive and what you would want it to be? If you cannot answer a strong "yes" to both of these questions, it is likely time for you to start taking steps to enhance your brand. Even if you said "yes" to both questions, I think that the concepts and examples in this book will encourage you to set your sights higher to realize your full potential.

Example 4: The Role of Student

When you are a student (college or high school), one of the things you must learn to do is network with people who can help you advance your career. With my students in college sport marketing courses, I encourage them to constantly think about their personal brand and to be strategic about making impressions that will allow people to speak on their behalf. When you are a student, you are sending a message about the type of professional that you are every single day that you go in to a class session. If you come in to class unprepared and do not pay attention to lectures/discussions, then you will likely come across as lazy and uninterested. Ultimately, this will make it unlikely the professor will be willing to write you an impactful letter when the time comes to apply for graduate school or jobs. This is also the case when you have guest lectures or when you get involved in practical work experiences. Approach these with the intention of going above and beyond so that you make an impression on the professionals you are meeting. With the right approach, you will build a brand that opens up opportunities for you as you move forward.

Example 5: The Role of Boss/Coach

As a boss or coach, your personal brand is important for a couple of reasons. First, it is your vision (and brand) that will provide a foundation for the type of organization/program that you will have in the future. In essence, you set the tone for the rest of the group based on your actions and your ability to model key values.

If you lead the right way, your personal brand will end up becoming a major part of the brand you are attempting to cultivate as a leader. Second, your actions will ultimately determine how your workers/athletes see you. If these actions are consistently positive and worthy of following, you will build a personal brand that will impact the people around you. If you make poor decisions, your relationships and your follower's perceptions of you will reflect this in a negative manner. You have the chance to be a leader that elevates your organization/program to a new level, but you have to make sure that you are making the right decisions on a daily basis to build a positive personal brand with your followers. It is absolutely critical that your actions are in alignment with your values so that integrity is a key part of your brand. Do this right and good things will happen.

We could go on and on with examples of roles where personal branding is important, but I think you get the point. Whenever we have interactions with people that matter to us, then it is worth our time to take a step back and think about how our actions influence their perceptions of us.

What Does This All Mean?

We all have different roles in our lives that have varying levels of importance to us. And yet, even in the ones that are an absolute priority, we rarely take the time to consider the influence we are having on others. While this is fascinating, it is not surprising when you consider the fact that our society seems to be cultivating a "me first" approach. The disappointing thing here is that this approach does not allow us to build meaningful relationships with others. Even with people who are extremely important to us, we lack the ability to see how our actions influence them on a daily basis because we are too focused on the outcomes for ourselves. This often places strain on our relationships and it negatively impacts our ability to build a unique personal brand with others. However, the good news is that we can change this quickly if we take the time to think about exactly who we want to become in our different roles, and how we can take steps to ensure that we realize our vision. By developing an approach that adds value to others, we will cultivate a personal brand that is conducive to success in all areas of our life. As legendary leadership guru Zig Ziglar said, "You can have anything you want in life, if you just help other people get what they want."

SO, WHO DO YOU WANT TO BE?

It is so important that you take the time to think about exactly who you want to be for others in your life. The last thing you want is to be the hypocrite parent, inconsiderate partner, crazy co-worker, selfish coach, lazy student or overbearing boss. The fact of the matter is that you may not even know that you are these things to other people if you are not taking the time to consider the implications of your actions. The first step to making sure that this does not occur is to reflect on your regular interactions and think about how they may be seen by others. Once you have done this, envision the type of person you would like them to see you as someday. Then, it is as simple as developing a plan to make sure you are consistent with your efforts to realize your vision.

SO WHAT'S NEXT?

At this point, you have made your initial assessment on whether or not you think personal branding can have an impact on your life. If this assessment has been positive, you will most likely read on and see how you can take steps to enhance your perceptions with others who are important to you. If this is the decision you make and you fully embrace the concept, I truly believe that you are taking the first steps to living a much more fulfilling life. Whether your goal is to be an amazing mother, classmate, coach, boss, sister or partner, personal branding can provide a framework to help you realize the brand vision that you have for yourself moving forward. Considering you are still reading, I will take it that you have made the wise decision to embrace this challenge. I am excited that I will be able to take this journey with you!

TAKE HOME POINT—
BE PROACTIVE ABOUT BUILDING BRAND

Now that you know you have a personal brand and that it impacts people around you on a daily basis, it is time to get down to business. Whether your decisions in the past have been good, bad, or indifferent, you can adopt a proactive approach and take control of the way that people see you today. With that being said, understand that it may take time to repair damage to relationships that happened because you neglected interactions with others in the past. However, if you are disciplined and persistent with your approach, you will eventually win people over and start to reap the benefits that come from living your life with a purpose and specificity. By making the decision to develop your personal brand today, you can cultivate an approach that regularly impresses people around you. First thing is first though. We need to develop an understanding of the core elements of personal brand so you have a foundation for making sound, impactful decisions on a daily basis. However, before we progress to these steps in the book, let's do a quick exercise that will help guide your efforts moving forward.

IMPRESSIONS IMPLEMENTATION EXERCISE

Several leadership experts have emphasized the importance of connecting with your mortality when striving to live an extraordinary life. One way to do this is by going through the "funeral exercise." In essence, this is when you close your eyes and visualize yourself at your own funeral. As you move towards the front of the funeral, some of the most important people in your life are there speaking about you. With this in mind, answer the following questions.

1. What exactly do you envision these people saying about you at the event? Be sure that you are extremely honest based on the way that you have treated them in the past.

2. Are you pleased with the things that you envision people saying about you? Is there anything that you would like to change about the message?

3. How are you going to go about creating change so that you are living the way that you would like other people to see you?

It is important to explain why we did this exercise at this point in the book. In addition to giving you a start on thinking about some aspects of your vision, this is a process that has many similarities to the branding process. By visualizing the ways that we would like people to see us, we can determine the type of personal brand that we would like to create in our life. If you are unhappy with your current situation, then make the decision to change your vision today.

CHAPTER 3

Vision is a Vital Starting Point in Branding

⁓

"Create the highest, grandest vision possible for your life, because you will become what you believe."

—*Oprah Winfrey*

At the core of all unique accomplishments in life is a vision that has driven great leaders to push way out of their comfort zones to do something special. This is exactly what Oprah Winfrey meant in the quote above, and this is certainly the case with individuals who build their brand in a unique manner. In many ways, there is nothing more important than taking the time to know exactly who you want to become in your life. This is something that few people take the time to do and as a result they are often unhappy with the outcomes that they are presented with in life. The truth is that you can minimize the chances of this outcome occurring if you simply take the time to really know the things about which you are passionate. This process certainly takes significant time and energy to reflect, but it is more than worth the investment because you are far more efficient down the road when you are working in your passion zone. Once you know the areas that inspire and motivate you, it is far easier to determine the goals you would like to accomplish in life and the career paths that will help you achieve them. Let's first start with the passion element, because it will directly impact the success you will have in all of the personal branding strategies that we will discuss throughout this book.

FINDING YOUR POINTS OF PASSION

It would be foolish to say that there was only one set way to go about finding the things you are passionate about. The reality is that you could ask 100 successful people how they realized their passions and you could get 100 different responses depending on your specificity. Some people are raised in households in which they are encouraged to chase their dreams at a young age. They have parents that talk to them about the things in which they are interested and they cultivate an environment wherein their children are able to experiment with their interests. And by doing this enough with structure, they often learn, through repetition and experience, what moves them. Others have had coaches and/or teachers that have challenged them to seek out their dreams and as a result have put them on the road to knowing what they are passionate about. With that being said, some of us have not been lucky enough to have individuals in our lives who have influenced us in this way. And even if we have had people who have done this for us, there is still sometimes uncertainty as to exactly what inspires us. This is all right because it is truly a tricky thing to iron out with everything going on in life.

The best way to learn the things we are most passionate about is through constant learning and reflection. For young professionals, this often involves getting involved in internship experiences so you can determine the things that you like and dislike. As you go through this process, you have the opportunity to actively assess experiences that help you to eventually determine the route you would like to travel. However, there is a step that likely even comes before this that can help with making sure we are moving in the right direction. One of the best ways to know the things that move you is by reading the right types of books on a daily basis. By simply investing 30 minutes each day reading leadership and development books, you can gain an understanding of yourself that you may not have had previously. The quality of content in these books is sound and they force you to reflect on the things that matter most to you. In addition, writing in a journal each day for 30 minutes reflecting on what you have learned each day is another way to ensure that you are constantly learning. As you recognize things that move you most (e.g., making a difference in people's lives), be sure to write them down so you keep track of areas that will eventually contribute to your list of values. In addition, within each of these areas, make a list of the people who you think best model these values and try to schedule a time to chat with them about their approach. For individuals who are successful, you will likely find that they have made decisions to live their life in passion areas. As a result, they are often both productive and happy because they are doing what they love on a daily basis. They might even tell you that they don't feel as though they have worked a day in their life because they are passionate about what they do.

WHO DO YOU WANT TO BE SOMEDAY?

This is one of the most important questions that you need to ask yourself. Who do you want to be someday? Another way of putting it is, what type of person do you want to be remembered as? These are powerful questions that have the potential to provide the clarity that you need to build a brand that will be meaningful and impactful for you down the road. The good news is that you already started to take steps to make this happen at the end of the last chapter with the funeral exercise. If you are not happy with the decisions that you have made in the past, then focus daily on who you would like to become and take consistent actions to realize this vision. We will focus on developing this for specific individuals/groups in a later chapter so keep things broad for now and envision how people will see you once you are living at your full potential. If this is unclear to you, then consider individuals who inspire you and write down the attributes that they have that you hope to embrace. Dream big here because you want a starting vision that will stretch you to be the best you can possibly become in the long run. At this point, it is perfectly all right if this is a specific position/role that you would like to be in down the road. However, if this is the case, then also visualize yourself doing the job so you know exactly what you are going to aspire to on a daily basis. After all, it doesn't do you any good to be in a unique position if you are not any good at it.

It is important to note at this point that it is perfectly all right if you do not immediately figure out everything when it comes to your vision for the future. In fact, it would be irregular if you did, because determining a vision is an ongoing process that unfolds as you develop as a person. Hopefully this book will help you take steps to make sure that this happens. However, in the meantime, there is nothing wrong with putting an initial vision in place that you can start to work towards. In addition to allowing yourself to learn more about this process and developing a personal brand, you will also take steps that will make you better as a person. The most important thing at this point is identifying some of your passions so you can put actions into place that will allow you to understand yourself much better as a person.

THE "WHY" IS EVEN MORE IMPORTANT THAN THE "WHAT"

As you consider who you would like to be someday, it is important that you take the time to dream big and to look for things that you believe will continually inspire you to grow in the distant future. Once you have done this, there is another step that is critical to take before you head off on your journey to chase your dream. While the "what" part of developing a brand vision is necessary, an even more important step is asking yourself "why" you are interested in pursuing your dream of choice. When this "why" is for the right reasons (and aligns with your passion and values), then there is a far greater chance of success down the road because it is something that deeply matters to you. If you do not spend the adequate attention and energy to get this right, you will likely end up losing interest at some point and the end result will be looking for an entirely new vision. Do yourself a favor and take the time to get this right so that you are a step closer to realizing your dream and full potential.

DON'T SETTLE FOR STATUS QUO

As you think about who you would like to be, don't be afraid to step way out of your comfort zone and visualize something that is far from being a reality at the moment. That is one of the purposes of vision. When done properly, it should stretch you daily to become something truly unique over time. This is one thing that differentiates highly successful individuals and people who are just average. The great leaders such as Walt Disney, Steve Jobs, Martin Luther King Jr., and Abraham Lincoln were all brave enough to believe in a vision that would impact the world far before it ever happened. While it is certainly not realistic for everyone to be this type of individual, it is reasonable to think that you can achieve unique things and leave your impact on the world. However, this will not occur if you allow your mind to get in the way when you are thinking about your passions and the vision that you have for your life. The key here is that you have to learn to truly believe in your ability to accomplish your vision. In fact, if you have a vision that is lofty enough, you will need to be so confident in your ability to achieve it that you will be able to fend off the criticism and frustration that will likely come during your journey. With a lofty enough vision, you will have others that will tell you that you are crazy and/or incapable, but it does not matter if you have chosen a vision that is in your passion zone and you are willing to put in the work on a regular basis. If you are not fully confident in your ability, then get to work daily studying on how to realize your vision. As you put in the time, the power of repetition will kick in and you will start to believe that you are capable of becoming the person that you hope to be someday. Another important element is regularly taking the time to visualize yourself achieving your vision. In combination with your other strategic repetitions, this will help your mind to believe that you are capable of achieving great things. This is all a part of realizing your full potential from a personal branding standpoint.

DARE TO DREAM: EXTRAORDINARY EXAMPLES OF VISION

If you want to be inspired when it comes to vision, you need to look no further than the individuals who have been willing to dream big in their pursuit to make their mark on the world. When you study great leaders, you quickly realize one thing that differentiates them from others is their ability to clearly see a vision far before it is a reality. This is in large part because they were willing to take the time to visualize who they would become and what they would accomplish in the early stages of their career/life. Studies by Harvard and Yale have actually shown that the small minorities of graduates (3%) who wrote down their goals out-earned the remaining (97%) of their fellow classmates. While money is certainly not the only measure of success, the concept can be implemented to other areas of success. The point is that you need to be specific about the things you would like to achieve so you can develop a focus on how you will achieve them. So, as we embark on this journey, why not focus on some extraordinary individuals who we can take lessons from that will encourage us to dream big and establish a vision that will inspire others around us? As you will find in these examples, it will also motivate us to add value to others as part of our personal brand. There is no coincidence that these great individuals left their mark on the world and are remembered because they placed a priority on inspiring others in some unique way. While they all went about it in different manners, their outcome is similar in their ability to make a difference.

—ABRAHAM LINCOLN—

Visionary Quote: *"That some achieve great success, is proof to all that others can achieve it as well."*

Vision Turned Reality: Abraham Lincoln's life is one that is known for both its adversity and for its legacy that it left on the United States. After failing at a wide range of professional endeavors (e.g., defeated for legislature, defeated for speaker, defeated for Senate, defeated for nomination for Vice-President), Lincoln remained persistent and became the 16th President of the United States.[1] He became the leader of the country during an extremely difficult time, forced to navigate the Civil War. But Lincoln knew what he believed in and felt strongly that slavery needed to be abolished in the United States. Despite extreme backlash from opponents, he was persistent in his actions and was able to lead the country through the Civil War and abolish slavery.[2] It is because of his brave passion that he made his impact on the United States forever, and as a result he is widely known as one of the greatest leaders that the country has ever seen. His success is seen as a unique example of what you can achieve when you pursue something with passion and persistence.

—MARTIN LUTHER KING—

Visionary Quote: *"Faith is taking the first step even when you don't see the whole staircase."*

Vision Turned Reality: Dr. Martin Luther King Jr. is a leader who is well known for his passion to achieve equality for African Americans in the United States. While other people were advocating for equality and freedom by any mechanism necessary, Dr. King went about his pursuit to realize his vision through non-violence and the power of words. Through his persistent daily actions, he was able to achieve great things because of his commitment to his values even in the face of extraordinary adversity. Known for his "I Have a Dream Speech" and for becoming the youngest ever to win the Nobel Peace Prize, Dr. King is credited for helping African Americans achieve racial equality in the United States.[3] It was his ability to believe in his vision that allowed him to take steps to realize an amazing legacy that changed the world.

—WALT DISNEY—

Visionary Quote: "*All our dreams can come true, if we have the courage to pursue them.*"

Vision Turned Reality: Walt Disney is an individual whose name is closely associated with creativity, innovation, and fun. With a passion for entertaining people and stretching the imagination, he was one of the best known motion-picture producers in the world. On top of this, his creative imagination and animation abilities led him to create legendary household charters such as Mickey Mouse, Donald Duck, and Pluto. Later in his career, he founded the Disneyland theme park that allowed children and families to experiences rides and to meet characters in one magical location.[4] It was his unique passion to give people a memorable experience that makes him one of the greatest entertainment innovators of all time. His vision led him to pursue this passion on a daily basis through the values that meant the most to him. Because of this, he was able to model his values and realize a brand that made a lasting impact on the people around him and across the world.

—STEVE JOBS—

Visionary Quote: *"If you don't love something, you're not going to go the extra mile, work the extra weekend, challenge the status quo as much."*

Vision Turned Reality: Steve Jobs is an individual who had a unique passion for business. Even more than this, he had a vision of creating electronic products that would change the way that the world operated through their ability to empower consumers. While Jobs' journey was more complex than we will explore here, he founded Apple and eventually helped turn it into one of the most powerful organizations in the entire world. However, what makes him truly unique is the fact that he had a specific vision that inspired him to create products that were simple, powerful, and aesthetically pleasing. It was his extraordinary passion that drove him to challenge the status quo on a regular basis, and as a result he was responsible for helping Apple to innovate while creating products such as the iPod, iPhone, iPad, and iTunes.[5]

HOW DOES THIS RELATE TO YOUR JOURNEY?

Some of you are probably wondering what these individuals have to do with personal branding. Well, the fact that you probably know about who they are and what they accomplished means that it has a lot to do with personal branding. Every single one of them had unique visions that they pursued with all of their energy over extended periods of time. And all of them had the unique ability to build relationships with people so that they would be on board to support their vision. It was their passion and pursuit that created energy around their cause that allowed them to accomplish things that will always be remembered in our society. In essence, their daily actions allowed them to build extraordinary brands over time because of what they were able to accomplish. However, there is a point here that needs to be clear when discussing these individuals. They are ordinary people just like you and I, but they had an extraordinary ability to dream and to chase those dreams down with discipline and passion. So, if you are looking to build a unique personal brand that will be remembered by people around you, then be willing to dream big and show your passion for your vision on a regular basis to the people around you. In the meantime, let's take a few minutes to digest some of the individual lessons that were presented from each of these outstanding leaders.

Lesson #1:
"The Proof That Others Can Achieve It"

The truth is that most people look at individuals who achieve great things and assume that they are just naturally gifted with extraordinary attributes. When you study these people, you quickly understand that one of the things that truly differentiated them was that they were willing to dream in a way that others were not. As Abraham Lincoln said, the fact that these things were done simply proves that others can achieve them. However, there is one thing that Mr. Lincoln left out and that is that you cannot achieve great accomplishments if you do not train your mind to believe that you can. The next time you start to envision something worth achieving and even have a hint of hesitation about your ability to achieve it, stop yourself and ask the question, "Why not me?" Get in the habit of believing that you are the type of individual that can set standards for others. Take the advice from Mr. Lincoln and be the one who provides proof to others that they can achieve something.

Lesson #2:
"Taking the First Step Without Seeing the Staircase"

While successful people develop the ability to see their vision in their mind, there are always uncertainties that come when you start to take steps to realize it. With lofty ambitions, you will normally not know what the exact next step is in your life, but you still need to be willing to move forward if you are going to reach your full potential from a branding standpoint. What the great Martin Luther King Jr. meant here is that you need to be willing to push forward even when you are not certain what comes next. Sometimes the best option is to take action and to learn from the process. And as you take these steps, you will start to figure out what your next moves are based on reflection and earned experience. But you have to be brave enough to move on your vision in times of uncertainty. The key here is to have faith that you are going to realize your vision and the top of the staircase regardless of what life sends your way.

Lesson #3:
"All Dreams Can Come True with Courage to Pursue Them"

When you find your passions and align them with your strength zones, you can achieve most things in life if your mind is right. Similar to Walt Disney, you need to have the courage to pursue them with everything that you have. You see, most people in life are scared to chase their dreams and as a result they never step out of their comfort zone. Many times, they are simply afraid of what other people will think of them when they learn about their aspiration or when they fail. Because of this, they never have the courage to stretch themselves and see what they can accomplish in life if they go all-in. When you have the courage to pursue your dreams, the one thing that you can guarantee is that you will always improve through repetition. Even if you don't at first realize your goals, you will move one step closer if you keep an open mind and learn from the process. Eventually, if you are persistent enough, you can achieve all of your dreams because you will have done something that 99% of people are never willing to do. They are not able to be courageous enough to chase their dreams.

Lesson #4:
"If You Don't Love It, You Won't Challenge Status Quo"

All of the great leaders that we have studied in this chapter have amazing legacies (brands) and have accomplished extraordinary feats because they chased their passions. These individuals pursued initiatives that they were inspired by because they dealt with making some kind of difference for people. For Lincoln and King Jr., it was about doing what was right to make sure that all people had equal opportunities. For Disney and Jobs, it was about creating products that could provide consumers with a unique experience that would enhance their lives. Because they were passionate about their cause, they were far more likely to challenge the status quo in their pursuits. As a result, they were able to do things that other people were never able to previously accomplish. The key here is that you must find goals and a vision that you absolutely love, so you are willing to chase it with a unique passion that will bring unique results.

IF YOU ARE NOT PASSIONATE, THEN REDIRECT . . .

There are so many people out there who are not happy with the way that they are living their lives. They are not passionate about anything and they simply go through the motions each day hoping for the next weekend to come. These individuals are always looking for something in the future (e.g., retirement) to come sooner because they believe their lives will eventually be better. And you know what happens when that thing comes? It usually isn't quite what they thought it would be (or it went by too quickly) and they are hoping for the next big thing. As a result, they are wishing away their life with nothing that really inspires them. If there is anything you take from this chapter, it is that passion is something that is worth pursuing. When you find it, you will be more energized on a daily basis and will find regular energy in your life. So, if you do not have things that you are passionate about, then make a change today. Take the time to learn about yourself and the things that really inspire you. When you start to realize what these things are, then arrange your life so that you can pursue these things on a daily basis through your relationships, position(s), and/or career. Life is far too short to wish it away and live far below your full potential. Create a vision for yourself that you are truly passionate about and then structure your life accordingly to make it happen. When you find clarity in your dream, then it is important to study what it will take to make it a reality. This is where the next step of putting your values into place comes in to play.

TAKE HOME POINT—
PASSION TAKES REAL PERSISTENCE

One of the biggest mistakes that people make is that they think passion is something that always comes naturally. As a result, when they do not feel a natural energy (momentum) for something, they tend to start thinking that it must not be their passion. The reality is that you have to work hard at being passionate. Life is not always easy and even if you are working at something you are passionate about, there will be times when you do not feel momentum. In these instances, you need to continue to move forward, reminding yourself of the reasons why you are chasing your passion. This is exactly why you must choose something that truly makes a difference. When you have chosen something noble and that matters to you deeply, you simply need to revisit these things and get back to the fundamentals (see values in next chapter). When you continue to live these values on a daily basis, you will eventually build momentum and you will strengthen your passion for your vision. Passion is something that takes discipline and it should be something that you pursue on a daily basis. Make it a part of your personal brand and strive to inspire others to live a life that is worth living. Do not be lazy and give up when something does not come easily to you. The greatest things in life (including passion) are ones that you need to work for over extended periods of time.

IMPRESSIONS IMPLEMENTATION EXERCISE

Building on the exercise you did in the previous chapter, close your eyes and envision yourself living the exact life you hope to live someday. Think about what you would like to do on a daily basis so that you would be energized and passionate to live well each day. Do this on a regular basis over the next week until you feel confident that you have a vision that you would like to pursue. While your vision will evolve as you move forward, this will give you a starting point with which to work. Once you have this set, ask yourself the following questions:

1. What exactly is stopping you from living your passion? How will you overcome these things so you can live a life that energizes you?

2. What are the things that you would need to do on a regular basis to realize your vision?

3. What types of things would you expect to slow you down as you pursue your vision? How would you overcome these things so you can progress towards living your full potential?

CHAPTER 4

The Virtue of Values: Creating a Structure to Realize Your Vision

❦

"Your beliefs become your thoughts, Your thoughts become your words, Your words become your actions, Your actions become your habits, Your habits become your values, Your values become your destiny."

—*Mahatma Gandhi*

Vision alone will not allow you to realize your full potential when it comes to personal branding. While it certainly provides an end goal and an initial passion for living, it does not provide you with the framework necessary to help you make decisions on a daily basis to realize your vision in the long run. This is where values come into play. Once you know your vision, the next step is to identify the things you will need to do to reach your full potential. More importantly, it will be imperative to know the values that you will embrace on a daily basis that are necessary to realizing your personal branding vision. This chapter is designed to help you with this process.

REVISITING THE WHAT, WHY AND HOW OF VISION

It is definitely possible that you may not determine your life-long dream of what you would like to achieve as you read this book.

However, you can certainly determine something that you would like to achieve in your life in the next 5-10 years. As we have discussed, this is the "what" in your strategic vision planning. On top of the "what," it is important that you examine the reasons "why" you would like to achieve this vision. This evaluation process is something that is critical because it will allow you to find something meaningful that will drive you when things get challenging. Hopefully, the earlier chapters in this book have got you initially thinking of the "what" and "why" of your vision so that you can start to create a path to realizing your full potential. Once you have done this, it is critical that you start to think of the things you will need to do to achieve the vision. This is exactly where your values come into play. These are the elements that you must embrace on a daily basis to ensure you are making decisions that lead you to living an outstanding life and also results in an extraordinary brand with others.

DEFINING VALUES

Values are the core beliefs and philosophies that are most important to us in our life. In simpler terms, they are the things that you value most in life that you can aspire to model on a consistent basis. Another way of putting it is that values should be meaningful reminders as to how you should live each day to realize vision and full potential. If you take the time to explore and determine the values that truly matter to you, it makes life far simpler because you know where you need to focus your attention and energy in branding efforts. In addition, when you get these values right, the steps you take moving forward will inspire you while also bringing a happiness to your life. You see, one of the only ways to truly feel content in your life is to live the way you know you should be living, even when you don't feel like living that way.

How To Determine Your Values

There are a few key steps that you can and should take to help identify your values. First, study other people that are successful and determine the things that they do on a daily basis to be successful. For this initial step, you should choose individuals you are inspired by because of their extraordinary influence that they have on others. Ellen Degeneres, who is a highly successful television entertainer and humanitarian had this to say about values: "Here are the values that I stand for: honesty, equality, kindness, compassion, treating people the way you want to be treated and helping those in need. To me, those are traditional values." If any of you have followed her career, you know that she absolutely models these values on a daily basis. As a result, she has an extraordinary, meaningful brand that has made her one of the most successful television personalities in the world. Equally impressive, she has achieved this level of success while earning the respect of pretty much everyone who interacts with her. With what she has accomplished, it would make sense to consider if some of the values she mentioned are a solid fit for you. They are certainly a reason why she has accomplished so much in her life.

The second way to help determine your values is by embracing a marketing mindset that we will discuss later in the book. If you want to identify core values that will enhance your life, consider the things that your key target markets value, and then determine whether they are meaningful to you. At this point, we can define target markets as people who are most important to you and/or people who have the ability to influence your career/life progression. For now, you can just briefly consider three because we will do this more in depth during Chapter #8. Once you have identified your key target markets, you will be far more prepared to strategically implement core values that allow you to make impressions and enhance your personal brand. In the meantime, pick one value from your research about an inspirational person and take steps to implement it in your life. For example, if kindness is something that speaks to you personally, then focus on being as kind as possible to people around you during the next week. This intentional approach will likely help you to improve in this area immediately because of your attention to make it a priority in your interactions.

The third and most effective way to cultivate the central core values that matter to you most is through reflection. The best strategy is to actively reflect on the things that give you sustained energy in life. However, please don't get frustrated in your first attempts to do this because getting to know ourselves well can take time. This is exactly why it is crucial to get in the habit of reading the right kind of books and listening to the right kinds of messages (e.g., podcasts, videos). There are so many amazing personal development experts such as Andy Andrews, Jon Gordon, John Maxwell, Jim Rohn, and Robin Sharma that will provide you with direction and inspiration when it comes to values and living the right type of lifestyle. If you spend enough time consuming the right kind of information, you will start to develop yourself, and your values will naturally come to the surface. This process alone is likely to teach you that one of your core values is "constant growth" because of the influence that it will have on your life.

Do Your Own Thing

There is no question that you should learn from others about values that may fit well into your life. After all, there are likely some amazing people living exactly the kind of life you would like to live from whom you can learn lessons. Even when you have values in place, there is a strong likelihood that you will make minor tweaks because you will learn from others and see opportunities to enhance your efficiency. With that being said, a point will come where you alone need to make a decision on the values that will work in your life. In your journey, there will be times where you recognize some "universal" core values (e.g., integrity, kindness, passion) worth implementing that are consistent among successful people you study. However, there will be other times when you reflect on certain values and determine that they are not the right fit for you. In this instance, follow your gut, because it is essential to choose values that you believe in during the personal branding process so that your actions come across as authentic (more on this in Chapter #7). When you move through this process and choose meaningful core values, it will be far easier to model them in a manner that will allow you to build solid relationships through your interactions. So, pick values that inspire you and be extremely passionate about making them who you are on a daily basis. This is the recipe for success in personal branding and in life.

PURPOSE OF VALUES IN SUCCESS

If your "what," "why," and "how" are in alignment, you have the necessary foundation in place to achieve success in your life. In essence, values are the "how" element of personal branding and they should serve as a direct path to your vision if you have the discipline to live them extremely well over extended periods of time. In addition to providing us with much needed structure, values are designed to be inspirational in nature because they stretch us daily to be a better person and to take steps towards our vision.

For example, if we happened to have a goal of becoming an Athletic Director at a top-tier Division I athletic department, it would make sense to cultivate an ability to connect with people, given that you need to lead a wide range of stakeholders. Thus, by choosing "connecting with people" as a core value, we can actively pursue this attribute on a daily basis so that it can become a skill set that comes more naturally to us. As a result of this investment, we move one step closer to our goal because of our enhanced ability to make positive impressions on people. The key thing to remind ourselves here is this will eventually become a part of our brand with others if we are persistent enough to chase it down on a daily basis.

How Values Influence Branding

As we mentioned briefly, values represent a necessary starting point for realizing our vision and personal brand in the future. Another way of looking at values is that they are the elements that we would like to become a part of our brand through consistent modeling. When you know the brand vision that you would like to realize, it simply becomes a matter of being great at consistently living your values during individual interactions with people. The ability to follow through on these values will ensure that your brand is closely aligned to the vision that you have in mind.

Values as Daily Checkpoints

One practical way of seeing values is that they are daily core philosophies that can serve as "standard of living" checkpoints. If being an energetic person is one of your core values, then you should assess how well you performed in this area at the end of each day. When you fall short of expectations, you should immediately develop a plan for how you will correct deficiencies the next day. If you are persistent with your efforts each day, it is simply a matter of time before performance improves and you start to model values in an efficient manner. Let's revisit our previous example to help illustrate this point. For Ellen, there is no confusion on how she should live each day because she has taken the time to know the values that matter most to her. With this clarity comes the ability to set standards for being great in core value areas so that she models them well every day. Equally important, this specificity allows Ellen to reflect on her performance on a regular basis so that she is able to grow in her value areas. Because her values are in alignment with her vision, they contribute to reaching full potential on a daily basis. This is exactly what you need to do if you want to be successful in the personal branding process.

TAKE HOME POINT—ADD VALUES TO YOUR VISION

Once you have a vision in place that is in alignment with your passions, it is essential that you develop a structure that will allow you to grow on a daily basis. Because our vision is lofty and requires significant investments, we need to consider the values that will allow us to maximize our potential in the future. As you strive to put your values in place, be sure to focus on choosing philosophies that are both inspiring and conducive to success. The good news is you can often identify "universal" values that successful people ahead of you have embraced in order to leave an extraordinary legacy. Study these individuals to see what makes them unique and then commit to making their most valuable attributes a part of your brand. With the right values, you can feel confident that you are well on your way to realizing your vision if you become a master at the modeling process. We will discuss exactly how to go about doing this in the next chapter. In the meantime, perform the chapter exercise to gain an understanding of some of the values you will work on modeling as we move through the steps in the book.

IMPRESSIONS IMPLEMENTATION EXERCISE

To help identify the values that will guide your personal branding process, go through the questions below and record your answers. While your values will certainly evolve as you read the rest of this book and beyond, it is critical to start examining the different attributes/philosophies that have meaning to you. Once you have done this, move on to the next chapter on becoming the master at modeling these values.

1. Spend time to identify three individuals who have attributes that you admire. These can be individuals you know personally or individuals who are having extraordinary success in your area of interest. Be sure to write these three individuals down and start to brainstorm what makes them unique.

2. Now that you have identified three individuals, what are the values that these individuals embrace to allow them to succeed?

3. Building on the previous question, which of these values would be beneficial to achieving the vision that you started to outline in the previous chapter? Write these down below and rank the ones that you are most passionate about as a person. This will start the process of identifying values you wish to make a part of your personal brand.

PHASE 2

Steps to Making an Extraordinary Brand a Reality on a Daily Basis

Implementation

CHAPTER 5

Master the Art of Modeling Values

⁓⊗⁓

"It is a matter of doing what you do best and not worrying what the other fellow is going to do."

—John Adams

In an earlier chapter, we touched on the importance of culti-vating a vision that would inspire and motivate us to reach full potential in the future. In addition, we discussed the concept of values and how they can help guide us to live in a way that will allow us to realize our full potential. These are the foundational elements for building an extraordinary brand. However, alone these mean nothing because you must take smaller steps to implement them if they are going to influence your life in a positive manner. As illustrated in the introductory quote by legendary world leader Mahatma Gandhi in Chapter #4, the process first starts with the beliefs and thoughts that you initially place into your mind.[1] If you take the time to know who you would like to become, you can visualize this daily and think about what it will take to become this type of person. When these are the thoughts that fill your mind, eventually your words and actions will fall into alignment and they will start to become habits. If done for an extended period of time, they become so engrained that they become core values that represent who you are as a person. However, this entire process takes discipline and persistence because you are responsible for taking action to set this process into motion. This chapter will emphasize some of the steps that are necessary to implement values so you can eventually realize your vision.

THE BASICS OF BRANDING AND MODELING

When you really break things down to a simplified form, branding is a fairly simple concept. If you take the time to know the values that are most important to you (with alignment in how you want people to see you) and you live them on a daily basis, you will maximize chances of building an extraordinary brand that can enhance all areas of your life. The key concept you must understand in order to achieve this reality is that branding is a daily pursuit in which you need to take control of your individual interactions. In addition to clearly knowing your values, this means you embrace those values to the point where they are a regular part of your daily living without even thinking about it. In essence, you have committed to living your daily value checkpoints so well over time that they simply become who you are as a person. If you have taken time to choose values that are important to key individuals in your life (and people in general), there is a great chance you will build solid relationships while cultivating a memorable reputation that will open up opportunities in your life. This is absolutely a process that is worth pursuing because it will allow you to impact the lives of the people around you.

CHOOSE VALUES THAT EVERYONE VALUES

The reality is that the personal branding process can be a little overwhelming because you are trying to identify the values that will best position you for future success. And as you consider the various things that are important to key individuals in your life, it can be confusing because there are so many things to consider. On top of this, you only have a limited amount of time each day to implement these values. The good news is, we will discuss streamlining this entire process for key target markets in Chapter #8. In the meantime, understand that there are certain values that are universally embraced by most people. For example, nearly all people you meet value integrity and being treated fairly during interactions. In addition, most individuals respond extremely well to people that add value to their lives on a daily basis. So, it would make sense to consider integrity and "adding value to people" as two of the key core values that will be a part of your personal brand. Once you have identified the universal attributes/principles that most people in life respond well to, you can make them core values that will serve as the foundation for your branding efforts. The key here is to become great at modeling them every single day so that they become a part of who you are when interacting with people.

LEARN TO "LIVE LIKE YOU ARE DYING" EACH DAY

When you know the core values that are most important to you and how to embrace them on a daily basis, one of the only things stopping you from realizing your vision is self-discipline and the ability to follow through on your intentions. The challenge is that this is not as simple as it seems until you have cultivated the right mindset to help you succeed. If you are fully committed to becoming a master at modeling your values, you need to learn to live exceptionally well one day at a time, to the best of your ability. One strategy that can be very effective here is to learn to live with a mindset that each day is your last. In essence, what this means is that at the end of each day, you should feel confident that you were great at living the values that are most important to you. When you "live like you are dying," you create a sense of urgency that gives you perspective and helps you to make sound decisions. If you do this extraordinarily well over time, you can establish habits that will ensure that you are leading a meaningful and impactful life.

BE EXCELLENT AT STRINGING DAYS TOGETHER

If personal branding is a new concept to you, the first step will be taking control of individual interactions with people. As we embrace this concept, the first major step will be learning to live single days extraordinarily well in key value areas. While this in itself should be considered an accomplishment, it is important that you realize that single days performed at a high level will do very little to establish a consistent brand with people. Because branding has to do with perceptions that are developed over time, it is important that you cultivate the ability to string well-lived days together over extended periods of time. Master this concept and you will build a brand that encompasses integrity because you will become known as a person who follows through on their intentions.

STRIVE TO MAKE YOUR VALUES A HABIT

Habits are formed by the actions you perform consistently over extended periods of time. When you make poor decisions and do not follow through on obligations and/or key initiatives, you will eventually become known as a person who lacks self-discipline. If this is done for long enough, this type of behavior can have devastating implications for your reputation and brand. On the flip side, when you are consistently disciplined about following through on these same obligations, you will eventually become a trustworthy person that others will want to be around. The same concept applies for connecting with people, being innovative, and pretty much any other value that you hope to master. The key here is to focus on areas in which you want to be strong and then to take steps to make sure that they become habits.

The process of developing habits often starts with setting immediate tangible outcomes that you can challenge yourself with on an hourly basis. If you have developed poor habits, you may need to first focus on eliminating negative thoughts so you can replace them with positive ones, an hour at a time. As you progress and feel comfortable with an hour, you can challenge yourself to extend the behaviors to half and full days. If you are persistent with your efforts, this will build up to the weeks and months that are necessary to form habits. However, it is important for you to understand that you may not succeed in achieving your outcomes as you move through your progression. When this occurs, assess the reasons why you may not have succeeded and quickly move on to strategies you can implement to improve your efforts. Do not dwell on the fact that you fell short of full potential as it will only limit your ability to realize the goals that you have set for yourself in personal branding.

REINFORCE HABITS THAT GOT YOU THERE

Once you have developed sound habits, there is no question that you will enhance the quality of interactions in your life. As you realize that this is taking place, it will be extremely gratifying because it will be the direct result of a hard earned progression. However, as you reach this milestone, remind yourself that this is not the time for you to relax and enjoy your success. As quickly as you adopted sound habits, you can bring poor ones back even faster if you get lax with your efforts. To avoid this, it is crucial to put a strategy in place that reinforces the right kinds of decisions. While you don't necessarily have to pay as close attention to every moment in your day, it is certainly important to reflect at the end of each day to make sure you are not allowing negative habits to resurface. One thing that can be extremely helpful is to write in a journal each day and focus on reflecting on your performance in key value areas. This is a good way to think back and determine whether you had any interactions that were not conducive to success. In addition, this will also teach you to have an open mind and to be on the lookout for any behaviors that are detrimental to your personal brand. It is easy to have blind spots where you do not see your deficiencies if you are not proactive about seeking them out and making them into something productive.

INCONSISTENCY IS DETRIMENTAL TO YOUR BRAND

As you move through the process of developing values that help you to build a unique brand, it is normal that you will have periods where you fall short of your performance expectations. After all, if you are a motivated person, you will likely continue to set higher standards that force you to continue to grow. In the times where you do fall short, it is important that you get back on track because inconsistencies can really hurt your personal brand. When you are saying one thing and doing something completely different on a consistent basis, then people will actually start to question your integrity or your ability to follow through on commitments. In either case, this can cause you to be perceived as the type of person that other people do not want to be around. The key here is to know your values and then be extremely consistent about living them on a daily basis. When you get this process right, you will develop a brand that is perceived as reputable because your words and actions will be in alignment. Equally important, the actual value areas on which you follow through will become a part of your brand as well.

TIPS FOR MASTERFUL MODELING IN BRANDING

Now that we have discussed the importance of modeling values on a consistent basis, it is time to break things down so you know the specific steps you can take when developing your personal branding plan. Building on the concepts covered so far in this chapter, this section will focus on giving you five tangible steps you can make instantly to ensure that you are implementing your values. Each of these steps are extremely practical and will allow you to realize your vision in personal branding if you follow through on them with discipline.

1. **Put Your Values in a Place that Is Visible**

    It can be easy to get distracted when there is a lot going on around us in our life. When there is constant clutter around us, you can easily deviate away from the values that are essential to realizing your vision in the long run. To avoid stumbles in your progression, make it a top priority to be in contact with your values on a daily basis. One of the best ways to do this is by spending at least five minutes each morning re-visiting your values prior to starting your day. In addition to staying connected to your values, it will get your mind moving in a proactive state because your values will likely be inspirational in nature. When first implementing your values, it is beneficial to look them over multiple times per day for five minutes. This can be as simple as placing them on a sheet that is right next to your bed so you can do it each morning and night. Placing them on the desktop of your computer is another way to make sure that you are capitalizing on repetition each day.

2. Invest in Strategic Reinforcement Initiatives

Seeing your values on a regular basis is the first step to make sure that you are moving towards full potential in personal branding. You know who you would like to become and are making sure you are reminded of this on a consistent basis. To help compound your efforts, it is very important that you spend time to reinforce your values by studying them. After all, if they are areas that are a top priority to you, then you should become an expert on them so you know how to make them a strong part of your brand. In addition, by studying them, you reinforce the values through the power of repetition.

3. Recognize that Repetition Is Your Friend

In sport, athletes invest in repetitions during practice each day so that they are able to become extremely efficient in their abilities. The concept is really no different for branding. Instead, you are focusing on areas that relate to normal living and you are "drilling" them daily so that you can become an expert in them. When you do this properly over time, the repetition helps you to ensure that you are a master at modeling the values that matter most to you. Given the implications of falling short, it makes sense to put a structure in place that maximizes your chances of fully embracing areas that will ensure success in your life.

4. Spend Time Learning from Other Masters of Modeling

As part of your progression, you should identify at least one individual who you consider to be an expert at modeling the values that matter most to you. Once you have this list, attempt to spend time with a few of these individuals at least once a month. When you reach out to them, you should tell them that you admire their abilities in a specific area and you would like to spend time with them to "pick their brain." If you are able to schedule a meeting with them, be sure that you take the time to write questions you would like them to answer in regards to the value area. When you meet with them, take notes so you can revisit key lessons on a regular basis. This part ties in to the repetition concept presented in the previous step.

5. End Each Day by Asking Yourself Simple Questions

One of the most important elements of personal branding is learning to reflect on your efforts on a consistent basis. It is a simple way to make sure we are on the path to realizing our vision in the future. One strategy to make sure this happens is by ending each day by asking ourselves a few questions. First, did you do everything you could possibly do to model the values that are most important to you? Second, did you find a way to build your personal brand with people who are most important to you? Third, if today were the last day on this earth, would you be happy with the way that you lived it? If you answered no to any of these questions, then you should revisit them and think about ways you can improve your efforts. Once you can answer yes to each of these questions, you are ready to move on to your next day. As you improve at this step, you will become far more efficient at living each day to your full potential.

SEEK OUT FEEDBACK TO ENSURE FUTURE GROWTH

As we touched on in the steps above, reflection is one of the most critical elements of branding. When you invest in initiatives to grow your brand, it is important to stop and reflect on whether you are living the values that are most important to you. In addition, you should also think about whether your actions are positioned well for the key groups of individuals in your life. To ensure that this takes place, don't be afraid to reach out to people around you to ask them for feedback. One of the best things that you can do is to find someone to whom you are close and ask them if they will provide you honest feedback on your daily actions. It is important that you encourage them to be open and that you will not get upset with them regardless of what feedback they provide. After all, if you are going to ask for it, you need to be ready to receive it even if it is not something you are pleased about. As a follow through, it is absolutely essential that you do not get agitated with them once you engage in this feedback process. If you ask for honest feedback and you receive it in an open, constructive manner, then you will get the type of suggestions that will allow you to be far more efficient with your brand-building initiatives.

ALWAYS HOLD YOURSELF ACCOUNTABLE

As you strive to realize your brand vision, it is essential that you learn to hold yourself accountable for your actions when they move in the wrong direction. When you fall short of your daily standards of living (as they relate to your values), be sure to acknowledge it and be persistent about getting right back on track immediately. While a single mishap is certainly not a big deal, you need to be careful to not allow it to happen consistently or it will become a counterproductive habit. If you do allow this to happen, it will become your new normal and eventually this will become a part of your reputation. The solution is fairly straightforward here. When you know how you should be living each day, be great at holding yourself accountable to the standards you have set in key value areas. And when you fall short, acknowledge it and recommit to living better the next day. As you learn from this process, you will get better at making sure that you are modeling your values extremely well.

TAKE HOME POINT—
MAKE MODELING VALUES A PRIORITY

One of the biggest challenges in personal branding is learning to hold ourselves accountable on a daily basis for modeling the values in which we believe. There are a lot of people out there who know how they should be living, but there are very few that have the self-discipline to follow through on their intentions. The individuals who become great at modeling the right values develop a unique brand that is perceived extremely well by others. The fact that their actions are in alignment with their words goes a long way in ensuring that they build trust with others. On top of this, they usually cultivate a reputation with unique perceived elements because their values have become a part of who they are in daily interactions. Knowing how to capitalize on this process is extremely empowering because it allows you to become the exact type of person you aspire to be in the long run. This is a powerful skill set that will afford you the opportunity to realize all of the dreams that you have in your life. But first, you must be willing to sacrifice so you will have the self-discipline to do the things that it will take to achieve something special.

IMPRESSIONS IMPLEMENTATION EXERCISE

With the five top values that you identified in the previous chapter, answer each of the following questions relating to becoming a master at modeling.

1. How can you feature your values in a manner that will inspire you to implement them (e.g., typed out to place in different locations)? Where will you strategically place these values to ensure that you see them on a daily basis for at least 5-minutes? Also, consider a consistent time in which you can study the values to embrace the power of strategic repetition. You are more likely to make this a habit if there is consistency in the process.

2. Who are the individuals that you can connect with to make sure that you are learning more about the values you hope to embrace in your life? What types of questions would you ask them if you were able to schedule a meeting with them?

3. What types of strategies (e.g., journal reflection on performance each night before bed) could you put in place to ensure that you are modeling values on a daily basis?

CHAPTER 6

Strive for Specificity in Branding Effort

⟨≈⟩

"Be a yardstick of quality. Some people are not used to an environment where excellence is expected."

—*Steve Jobs*

We have touched on the fact that everyone has a personal brand, but you may still be wondering exactly what this means. Let's start by using an example that illustrates the concept of branding. In the sport industry, brand is characterized by the thoughts that come to mind when a consumer comes in to contact with the name, colors, and/or marks that are associated with a sport organization. It is easy to argue that the brand also extends to coaches and athletes who are highly visible in the media. For an athletic department like the University of North Carolina, this means that all interactions that come from their department either add to or detract from their brand. So, when someone comes in to contact with the NC logo or the "Carolina Blue" colors, they intuitively have thoughts that come to mind based on past experiences and/or interactions with the athletic department.

Marketing guru Seth Godin adds that much of an entity's brand is made up of a "set of memories, stories and relationships that, taken together, account for a consumer's decision to choose one product or service over another."[1] According to this definition, it seems that much of a brand has to do with the unique relationships that organizations are able to build with their followers based on the experiences they are able to create. When these are personalized and/or special for followers, you are able to create a brand that consumers are loyal towards. If this happens, then you often reap the benefits of word-of-mouth advertising because highly satisfied consumers will tell their friends about their experiences. When this occurs, you have created a brand that is unique enough that people want to talk about it, and this often opens up opportunities that bring new benefits to the organization.

How To Make Brand Personal

We have already illustrated that brand has to do with the thoughts that come to people's minds when they come in to contact with an organization, and that previous decisions by the organization help shape exactly what these perceptions are for individuals. With this foundation in place, the concept of personal brand is fairly straightforward. In essence, it is the thoughts that come to people's minds when they come in contact with you, or when they come in to contact with some of the materials/products you have created. Similar to organizational branding, these perceptions are largely determined by the decisions that you make on a daily basis when interacting with people. The great thing about personal branding is that it is far less complex than organizational branding because you are only dealing with decisions made by one individual: You. In theory, this means that a personal brand is much easier to control because it is not influenced by other people's decisions that are connected to your organization.

APPLYING THE CONCEPT OF BRANDING WITH APPLE

To further illustrate the concept of personal branding, it is useful to provide examples of entities that have built remarkable brands. What better way to do this than by examining one of the most successful brands in the entire world. This is a brand that is widely recognized as being innovative and has changed people's lives through the products that it has created. You may have even guessed by this description that we are going to be talking about Apple. The multi-billion dollar question is what exactly is the Apple brand made up of and how did they get to the point where they are the top brand in the world? While the answer certainly involves a wide array of elements and contributions that we will not cover in this book, there are some key central elements that have differentiated the company from competitors and have positioned them effectively for consumers. By first examining these elements in an organizational setting, we can gain a better understanding of concepts that can be highly effective for you in personal branding initiatives.

IT'S ALL ABOUT APPLE

Similar to most other organizations, Apple's core brand is made up of its name, logo, colors and/or marks. These are generally the most fundamental areas that people encounter which make them think of Apple's brand. However, it is important to recognize that this is only a small part of branding because a large part of consumer's perceptions have to do with decisions that Apple makes on a daily basis to position their organization. These are brand extensions, and for Apple this has included key elements such as: (1) vision, (2) products, (3) marketing, (4) customer service, and (5) creative bundling. These are areas we will discuss briefly before touching on how they influence personal branding.

1. **Vision.** One of Apple's greatest strengths is their ability to narrow in on a few values that guide their actions on a daily basis. As demonstrated in *Steve Jobs* by Walter Isaacson, Apple has focused sharply in on three primary values that dictate their approach in all key business decisions: Innovation, simplicity, and user friendliness.[2] Their pursuit of innovation has pushed them to create products that have transcended the technology field (see next branding element for specific examples). In addition, the passion that Steve Jobs had for making products simple and user friendly has been something that has allowed Apple to become a household name. With these values, Apple has created a specificity that has allowed them to become the number one brand in the world with a value of $104.3 billion.[3] The key point here is that this extraordinary brand has been guided by set values that were determined far before the success that is being realized today.

2. **Product.** To be efficient in branding, you must have a product that is positioned specifically for your key target markets (audiences). For Apple, they have developed a string of products that have added value to the lives of consumers all across the United States and the world. This started with the creation of a personal computer to empower consumers

and it has extended to the iPod, iPhone, iTunes, iPad, and a variety of different products that are now common "household items." By developing unique products that add value to consumers, they have differentiated themselves in a manner that has made their organization truly great. In terms of developing a differentiated product, sometimes this takes following Steve Job's philosophy of showing people what they want before they even know it. This is what innovation is all about.

3. **Marketing.** There is no question that having great products alone will not guarantee an extraordinary brand. The truth is you must have sound marketing strategies in place to ensure that your products are seen favorably in the minds of consumers. Extending from the previous element, marketing is influenced by the visual appeal of the product from the time consumers see it in advertisements to when they come into contact with the product "in person" for the first time. If you have ever seen an Apple product display, you know they have taken extreme steps to ensure that it has a clean and inviting appearance. Much of what Apple invests in is making a unique impression that adds to the experience for consumers during their purchase. This is reinforced by the emphasis that Steve Jobs placed on the packaging for Apple products. The innovative advertisements in the past have also helped build the Apple brand in the minds of consumers. The point is that the organization has gone out of their way to position their products in a unique way that has turned consumers into self-proclaimed "Apple people."

4. **Customer Service.** As an extension of branding, Apple's customer service involves the one-on-one interactions with consumers that take place on a regular basis. Another way to look at this is that Apple makes sure that employees are able to build strong relationships with consumers. While there are a variety of factors to consider here, much of this process is characterized by the help their employees provide to consumers throughout the product cycle (before, during, and after making a purchase). When this is done in a manner in which the consumer's needs are placed first (within reason), there is a chance to build loyalty that adds unique value to the organization. The "Genius Bar" is one example of how Apple has created customer service that has cultivated loyalty with consumers.

5. **Creative Bundling.** In addition to high quality products, the brilliance of Apple's business plan is that their products are so compatible with each other. On top of this, they have revolutionized the music industry with their iTunes model. However, it is the overall compatibility between their products (devices, apps, and iTunes) that makes what they do so effective. The bundling makes the experience seamless for consumers and in the end provides a better overall product that builds the Apple brand. In essence, they have taken different products with compatible uses and combined them in to one system to fit their innovation, simplicity, and user friendly values. In the end, they have done an outstanding job developing a variety of products that are created to add value to their consumers.

6. **Above and Beyond Mentality.** When you combine all of the unique elements discussed above, you can see how Apple has created a unique, one-of-a-kind brand. They have gone above and beyond to add unique value to people's lives and this has allowed them to "leave their dent in the universe." It is the pursuit of this impact that guides all extraordinary branding efforts and is something that should be noted. The underlying principle is a real passion to do something special.

IMPLICATIONS FOR INDIVIDUALS

As you may have already guessed, one of the things that makes Apple unique is their specificity in their branding efforts. They know exactly who they want to be and they make decisions that fall into alignment with their values. As a result, they are delivering the types of products and experiences that build their brand in the minds of consumers. Relating to individuals, the concept of personal branding is very much the same, but it focuses on the specificity in efforts created by you. In essence, as we have discussed in previous chapters, you should take the time to know exactly who you want to be far before you start to cultivate your brand. For the time being, why not apply some of Apple's strategies to our own personal branding efforts?

1. **Vision.** Similar to Apple, success in personal branding starts with a vision that guides all of your actions and decisions on a daily basis. We have said this multiple times already in this book, but it is worth mentioning again because it is such an important step, and repetition is our friend. If you are in a field in which creativity and innovation are highly valued,

then make these your values and strive to embrace them at every opportunity. If people are important to you, then place connecting with others at the top of your priority list and focus on building relationships on a daily basis. The point is that you must have a clear vision so you know how to live on a daily basis. When you take control of individual interactions by living your values, you provide yourself with the opportunity to build a personal brand that is meaningful and impactful, that is, if your values are chosen wisely for the life you hope to live.

2. **Product.** When I work with individuals, one of the most interesting concepts for them to embrace in personal branding is that they need to see themselves as a product. Simply put, Apple is a great organization because they have outstanding products they have developed to sell to their consumers. While a slightly different context, this is really not different for individuals. If you want to open up opportunities in your life, then you need to cultivate skill sets that will differentiate you from others. For most individuals, you will be seen as a product when you are applying for jobs or seeking promotions. When you develop a strong product tailored to the unique needs of your environment, you increase your chances of developing a personal brand that is conducive to advancement.

3. **Marketing.** Apple has great products that have the potential to impact people's lives on a broad scale. However, this does no good if people do not know anything about Apple. This is why Apple has made strategic decisions to make sure that

messages are spreading about the quality of their products. Similarly, individuals must develop a strategy that ensures that key individuals see the skill sets they have developed. This is a primary reason why young professionals are taught to develop job application materials that allow them to shine. In addition to the visual appeal, the way that expertise and skill sets are portrayed go a long way in determining a first impression for interested candidates. For individuals already currently in positions but are looking to advance, this involves developing the types of presentation that have a "wow factor" for the key people around them. Remember, your skill sets are critical foundational elements, but they mean little if you do not develop the ability to showcase them for people. Learn to do this extraordinarily well and opportunities will open up for you.

4. **Customer Service.** The reality is that the foundation of customer service is about putting people first. Apple has placed a high priority on this and so should you. When you strive to develop relationships with people in a unique way, you cultivate a brand that shows people that you care about them. With this approach, you are far more likely to be seen as a quality person, resulting in loyalty with others. However, it is important to note that this will not work for you if your interest in others is insincere. While some folks will say that being kind is weak, developing a customer service mindset will do nothing but bring positive results if you do it the right way. I would argue that putting people first is at the core of all successful branding initiatives. Considering that personal brand is determined by other people's percep-

tions, it is difficult to build a productive image if you are not able to see things from others' viewpoint. It is this proactive approach that will allow you to eventually become an expert in personal branding.

5. **Creative Bundling.** As we mentioned, one of the things that makes Apple unique is the fact that they have so many products that work well together. They have creatively bundled these in a way that makes the user experience unique for consumers. So, how does this relate to individuals? Well, if you are looking to make an impression in a specific area, you can develop skill sets that work well together and differentiate you from others. For example, if you work in marketing, you can make yourself unique by cultivating skill sets in graphic design, social media, and/or video production. By gaining an understanding of key marketing areas, you can increase the chances of being valuable to the organizations (or individuals) that you are targeting. This is the case in any area of your life in which you are trying to build your personal brand with people. The ability to create a well-rounded product that adds value to others will always be a smart investment.

TAKE HOME POINT— BRANDING WILL BUILD REPUTATION

By now, my hope is that you have an understanding of why personal branding matters, and that you are committed to making decisions that will maximize efficiency of interactions on a daily basis. If not, then know that it is a meaningful endeavor because it increases your chances of success in the areas of life that matter to you most. By developing an awareness of personal brand, you can make decisions that will intentionally build relationships with the people around you. There is no question that the right proactive mindset allows you to make sure you are treating people in a manner that will leave a lasting impression. When you do this consistently well over time, you not only strengthen relationships, you also develop a reputation for which people are willing to step up and vouch for you. In addition, you can strategically invest in initiatives that will develop skill sets conducive to achieving the unique goals that you have for your life. The bottom line is that embracing personal branding concepts will help to open up opportunities in your life. You will be taking steps towards full potential and this is something that is a rewarding endeavor in itself.

IMPRESSIONS IMPLEMENTATION EXERCISE

If we pay attention to our interactions with companies, we can learn a lot about branding strategies to implement in our lives. The truth is that companies/organizations are far more evolved than individuals at branding because it has been a more common emphasis for entities looking to maximize profits. Consequently, it can be useful to think about our experiences with companies/organizations that we have had recently. Based on these reflections, answer the following questions:

1. Are there any memorable negative experiences that you have had recently with organizations? If yes, write down exactly what made them negative for you. If not, pay attention in the next week and finish this step as you have a negative experience.

2. Are there any memorable positive experiences that you have had recently? If yes, write down exactly what made them positive for you? If not, pay attention in the next week and finish this step as you have a positive experience.

3. Are there any specific lessons you can learn from these experiences that you can apply to your own personal brand? Be sure to write these down and to strongly consider ways in which you can avoid the negative and emphasize the positive.

CHAPTER 7

Aspire for Authenticity in Daily Interactions

⁓

"To be yourself in a world that is constantly trying to make you something else is a major accomplishment."

—Ralph Waldo Emerson

The ability to learn to be yourself is one of the most important steps in your progression to build an extraordinary brand and life. If you take all of the previous steps and choose values that you do not believe in, you will eventually fail because your intentions will come across as inauthentic. There is nothing worse in branding than coming into contact with someone who has intentions that seem fake. To avoid this, you need to constantly make sure that there is alignment between your values and your daily actions. The goal is to develop a brand in which people see you as real, and being consistent in your words and actions is the first step to making this happen. This chapter will be dedicated to helping you understand some of the key steps to developing an authentic personal brand with others.

Don't Be THAT Person

Every one of us can probably remember at least one person we have encountered who has had regular inconsistencies between what they say and what they do. While we are all guilty of doing this occasionally on a smaller scale, these people spend their days talking a big game and rarely do anything to back it up. Have you ever met someone who claims to be all about something and then does the exact opposite in their actual actions? My guess is we probably all have. The problem with this approach is that it usually upsets the people around them and as a result they are not trusted. For some folks, this might have been the boss that talks about putting in extra time at the office to get things done and then leaves work early to go golf with friends. Or this could be the teacher that tells students how important it is to demonstrate professionalism by coming to class prepared and then comes in late and unprepared for lecture. We can all relate to how we feel when people don't follow through on the things they say are important. Spend enough time to think about how you feel about these people and it will likely be enough to inspire you to be a person of your word. Don't be the person who lacks authenticity in their actions. Get to know who you are and hold yourself accountable for the things that truly matter to you.

Get To Know Who You Currently Are

It is difficult to ensure that you are developing an authentic brand if you have not taken the time to know who you are and what matters to you. The good news here is that you have already spent some time developing an understanding of these elements by exploring your passions, vision, and values in earlier chapters.

When you are able to clearly understand what these things are, then you will know what type of person you would like to become. As we have previously discussed, then it is a matter of putting a structure in place that allows you to implement these things on a daily basis. However, there is also value in knowing the person you are at the moment so you can make sure you are not straining relationships with inconsistencies in your words and actions. While we might love to be a selfless person that puts other people first, it is possible that we still have some selfish habits that we are working on eliminating. In this case, we want to be careful about portraying this as a well polished attribute to the people around us because it will come across as inauthentic through our selfish actions. The best thing to do here is to consider it an aspirational value and acknowledge that it is something that you hope to fully embrace in the future. By knowing who we are, there is a far greater chance that we will continue to develop a personal brand that is strengthened by the people around us.

ACKNOWLEDGE GAPS IN WHO YOU ARE AND WHO YOU WANT TO BECOME

For most motivated people, there will always be a gap between the person they currently are and the person they want to become. Even when you are making progress and embracing values, you will often set new standards to strive for as you invest in personal development activities. If you are constantly pushing to be better, then these gaps are a good thing because they are a part of your growth plan. However, as we look at the key areas in our life that are most important to us, we should take at least an hour each month to assess the gap between where we are and where we want to be for each of our values. For example, if you are aspiring to be a person who is positive and does not complain, you should be able to determine how well you are doing this on a daily basis through this process. You can use your notes from journaling and feedback from others to assess performance in each area. It is important that we have an awareness of effectiveness in each of these values because it will directly influence the perceptions that others have of us. While it seems like a small thing, your authenticity is influenced a great deal by this process and you cannot reach full potential in relationships if people do not believe that you are a person of your word.

DON'T FAKE IT TO TRY TO MAKE IT

There is nothing wrong with having areas in our life in which we are not excellent. In fact, it is likely we will all have areas in which we are not performing to our full potential. However, there is absolutely a problem with pretending that we are something we are not. For some reason, we have been taught (even if indirectly) to pretend we know the answers to questions we do not know. Rather than admitting that we don't know, we often try to make things up so that people will think we are important and/or smart. I have to admit that this was something I felt I had to do when I first started teaching at the college level. Whenever a student asked a question I was unsure of, I tended to believe they would think less of me if I was not able to answer it right away. As a result, I was responding with information that was far less effective than they deserved. In addition to potentially leading people in the wrong direction, the problem with this approach is that most people can see right though this if they are around you long enough. When they see this, they are far less likely to take you seriously because they will perceive you as ineffective and/or inauthentic. With experience, I have learned to just admit that I do not know the answer, but that I would look into it to see if I could provide some insights at a later time. I have come to realize that there is absolutely nothing wrong with this because nobody has all the answers to the questions that are presented to them. As a leader, I now know that this is the right approach because it models being real to the students and professionals that I work with on a regular basis.

LEARN TO JUST BE YOURSELF

Think about the people in your life that you really love to be around. What is it about these people that make them unique? While they likely have sound attributes and values, it is almost certain that they are also just down to earth people who are comfortable with who they are. If you want to be this type of person with an associated authentic brand, then you need to learn to just be yourself. This is even the case if you are in a place where you are not happy with your current skill set and brand. It is far better to have gaps in a variety of skill sets and acknowledge them than to have few gaps in skill sets and not acknowledge the few that you have. Most people can appreciate you being far less than perfect if they know that you are aware of your shortfalls. It is important to point out here that you are not accepting the shortfalls that you have in key areas in your life. Rather, you are acknowledging them and pledging to improve them by living the right way. In the process, you are cultivating an authenticity in your brand because you are far more likely to come across as real when you acknowledge your short falls and stop pretending you are something that you are not. Through this process, it will make it far easier to be alright with who you are as a person so you can embrace being yourself. While this may not occur immediately, hopefully this book will serve as a guide to help you achieve this mindset.

DON'T HOLD OTHERS TO A HIGHER STANDARD

We have already touched on the issues you can encounter in personal branding when there are incongruences between your words and your actions. In essence, we are not following through with the things that we portray as being important and this can cause issues with the relationships we have with others. However, there is another thing that causes far more resentment with others when it comes to this process. While most people can be a little critical when others do not follow through on their words, they are far more likely to get upset with you if you hold them to a higher standard than you hold yourself. If you talk about the importance of treating others well, people are likely to get more than a little agitated if you get in the habit of publicly criticizing others. When you make this decision and let yourself off the hook while criticizing others for the same behavior, there is a good chance they will take it personally and resent you for it. If you want to build a unique brand with other people, there is a simple formula to follow here. Hold yourself to a unique standard of excellence that others will see on a regular basis. If there are things that matter to you, then strive to be outstanding at modeling them on a regular basis. Be absolutely sure that there are real congruencies between your values and actions. Make sure that this is so engrained in who you are that you are always holding yourself to a higher standard than you hold others. By doing this, you will minimize the chances that others react negatively to you because you will be modeling the things that you value. While they may not agree with these values, most people can respect your decisions because you won't be asking them to do something that you are not willing to do yourself.

STAY AWAY FROM BEING CRITICAL OF OTHERS

I have to admit that being critical of others has been one of my biggest weaknesses when working with people. And I can honestly say that there have also been times when I have been critical of others while holding them to higher standards than I was holding myself. The good thing is that once I acknowledged these weaknesses, I was able to make adjustments to make sure I was being less critical of others while holding myself to a higher standard. The mistake you make when consistently being critical of others is that you get in the habit of focusing on their perceived weaknesses rather than their strengths. When you get in this habit, you often treat people in a manner that is not conducive for building relationships with them. And when "adding value to others" and "being positive" are two of your core values, then there is a strong chance you will have incongruences that will hurt your relationships with others. On top of this, the criticism of others (especially when they are not around) will bring a negative element to your brand that will limit your potential. In addition to detracting people from wanting to be around you, they will be less likely to trust you because they will become skeptical of your approach. After all, if you will talk about all kinds of other people while they are not around, why wouldn't you talk about them in this manner as well? This is a habit that has extremely negative consequences and it is one that you should avoid if you are pursuing the development of a unique brand that adds value to others.

TIME WASTED ON NEGATIVITY EQUALS TIME NOT BUILDING

There is no question that criticism of others alone has negative consequences in the personal branding process that are worth avoiding. However, there is another reason why you need to be diligent about avoiding negativity in your daily interactions. Here is something to consider. The National Science Foundation estimated that we spend up to 80% of our days on negative thoughts.[1] For every minute that you spend being critical of others or a situation, you lose a minute that you could spend on developing your personal brand. So, if we have negative thoughts at this rate during a 16-hour awake period, this means we are wasting up to 12.8 hours per day and 4,672 hours per year on these thoughts that could be used to move towards full potential. While this can certainly vary from person to person, the point is clear that we waste significant chunks of time on these negative thoughts. Simply understanding this alone is enough to make you want to be diligent about eliminating negativity from your life. This is a step that will differentiate you from others in your personal brand.

TAKE HOME POINT—ASPIRE FOR AUTHENTICITY

One of the keys to branding is to find an approach in which you come across as an authentic person. I am sure you can attest to the fact that people do not want to be around individuals who come across as fake or inauthentic. This is why it is so important to know your values and who you would like to become someday, so you can work on being yourself around others. When you know these things, it is far easier to make daily decisions that will allow you to eventually realize your brand vision. In this process, it is critical that you hold yourself to a unique standard that will allow you to build relationships with the people around you. Remind yourself that a key part of authenticity is learning to hold yourself to a higher standard than you expect of others. With this philosophy, we will be far less likely to be critical of others and we will instead spend our time on building a personal brand that will be valuable to the people around us.

IMPRESSIONS IMPLEMENTATION EXERCISE

We all have times in which we do not follow through on the things that we determine as essential to our lives. It is human nature to slip up from time to time and to not live up to our own standards. To make sure we are cognizant of these instances, get in the habit of asking yourself these questions on a weekly basis to keep yourself accountable. Go ahead and do this now to get in the habit of meaningful performance reflection.

1. For each of your top five value areas, rate your current level of effectiveness on a scale of 1 to 10 (with 1 being extremely poor and 10 being outstanding). Once you have done this, reflect on the gap between your current performance and where you would like to be in the future.

2. What steps/strategies can you implement to make sure that you reach your full potential in each of these areas moving forward?

3. Are there recent instances where you have held others to a higher standard than you hold yourself (or simply have been critical of others)? Are there any implications on your personal brand if you maintain this behavior?

4. For one hour in your day, write down any instances in which you catch yourself focusing on a negative thought. Once you have finished this hour, reflect on these instances and determine how you can limit these thoughts moving forward so that you are able to cultivate a positive brand.

CHAPTER 8

Be Mindful That Branding
IS NOT All About You

❧

"If an individual is compassionate and altruistic, and has the interests of others in mind, then irrespective of whether that person knows a lot of people, wherever that person moves, he or she will immediately make friends."

—Dalai Lama

The tricky part of branding is that the initial movement always starts with you, because you are developing a vision based on where you would like to go in life. In many ways, this starts as a selfish initiative because we are all motivated to some extent by the ability to enhance our lives and increase our chances of success. There is nothing wrong with this as long as it is controlled and guided in the right direction. You see, even with selfish motives in mind, branding must have to do with others if you want it to be a successful endeavor. Given that branding is guided by the perceptions that others have of you, it is not reasonable to think you will succeed if you do not learn to see things from other people's viewpoints. This chapter is going to be dedicated to helping you understand this concept. By the end, it is my hope that you will have adopted a "marketing mindset" that allows you to identify your key segments and consider their wants and needs. At minimum, you must have a "people first" mindset in which you learn to add value to the key people in your life (or at least have them think you can add value to them if they are distant contacts).

MAKE THINGS ALL ABOUT OTHERS

One of the biggest challenges in traditional marketing (and branding) is that people have a difficult time seeing things from other people's perspectives. Yet this is exactly what it takes to succeed in marketing because you must be able to position your product so that folks are inspired to consume it with their hard earned money. When most professionals get involved in a marketing position, they often make the mistake of developing strategies solely based on what they think is interesting. As a result, they develop and/or release a product that is not positioned well for the key individuals they are targeting. Then, through a series of failures, they slowly learn that they must develop the ability to make things about others if they want to succeed in creating interest for their product. Through successes, they are reinforced with the fact that a "people first" mindset is necessary to create a unique brand that creates loyalty with consumers. This is no different in personal branding. To be successful, you must consider the individuals who you would like to impress and then think about how you can go about doing that (from their perspective). It is your choice whether you do this up front or if you need to fail like the other marketing professionals we mentioned. My suggestion would be to develop an ability to make things about others today and choose the quicker path to success.

AN "ALL IN" BRANDING MENTALITY

Personal branding is not a part time endeavor in which you turn things on and off depending on who you are around. If you want to be authentic and as efficient as possible, your personal branding becomes a lifestyle that you embrace regardless of who you come in to contact with. The reality is you simply cannot know when you are meeting someone with the capability to help you in some area of your life. And to be honest, this should never be your primary focus if you are hoping to build a unique brand. The point here is you should strive to make a unique impression on every single person that you meet. If you embrace this concept and live the right values on a daily basis, your brand will simply become an extension of who you are as a person. On top of this, your actions allow you to build relationships with individuals who believe in your skill sets and the way you are living. So, if you want to build a unique, differentiated personal brand, then plan on going "all in" with your efforts and making it a lifestyle. This is the only real way to realize full potential in your life.

BECOME A MASTER AT MAKING AN IMPRESSION

Building on the previous section, individuals who are outstanding at personal branding learn to master the art of making an impression. Simply put, they are passionate about doing everything in their power to live as well as they possibly can, and they strive to make the most out of opportunities to build relationships daily. It is not a gimmick, it is simply who they are because they are passionate about setting a unique standard through their actions. For these individuals, every single interaction that they have with people is one in which they want to make an impression. By taking control of these small, seemingly inconsequential interactions, they continually make investments that add up to something truly remarkable from a personal branding standpoint in the long run. Eventually, their efforts pay off and opportunities open up because they valued interactions and constantly impressed the people they came into contact with. If we think hard enough, we all know someone who is like this and they are the type of person we want to be around because they make us better people. That is exactly what you should strive for if you want to build a unique personal brand. Make it one of your values to add value to people as often as possible.

THE SECONDARY STRATEGY: CAPITALIZE ON SEGMENTATION

If you want to be great in personal branding, you should put your efforts into mastering the art of making an impression, as touched upon in the previous section. However, there are certainly times when targeting specific groups makes sense because it allows us to be more efficient with our efforts. Given that life is so busy, sometimes we simply have to make a choice about whose lives we are trying to add value to through our interactions because we do not have the time to do it for everyone. This becomes increasingly more true as we improve at adding value to others because you will have more people requesting your time. In this instance, you must learn to prioritize the importance of individuals in your life. In marketing, this is called segmentation and it involves the identification of key target markets that potentially have an interest in your product. This concept is very much the same in personal branding, but you are instead initially envisioning the individuals (or groups of individuals) on whom you hope to make an impression through your interactions. Once you have identified these key individuals, it is critical to take the time to think about the primary interests of these segments so you are able to make decisions to position yourself moving forward. Finally, you should determine the specific strategies you will act on to build your personal brand in a unique way in the future. Each of these steps will be discussed prior to moving on to specific strategies to take control of your brand.

1. Identifying Key Target Markets

It does little good to invest in the branding initiatives that will be discussed in this book if you have not taken the time to know the individuals who will be key to realizing your goals and vision. There are two different ways to look at this strategy. First, as we have briefly touched on, there is the view that you should strive to make an impression on everyone you meet and/or interact with because you absolutely never know who will be in a position to add value to your life. This would certainly be the gold standard of personal branding because it encompasses treating every person well and strives to build relationships as often as possible. The second view is that you should identify specific individuals and/or groups in strategic positions with the capability to help advance your career or life so you can develop strategies to make an impression on them. So, which view here is most effective? The answer is that you can use both to maximize personal branding initiatives. If you want to build an elite level brand, then you should work to set a standard of excellence as often as possible so you are always impressing people through your actions. However, this does not mean that you should not strategically consider individuals with the potential to help you. In fact, this is something that would be smart to do if you want to be more efficient with your efforts. Because you have limited time in a day, the identification of key individuals allows you to know where to place your emphasis so that you can make strategic impressions that will advance your career.

With the previous comments in mind, it is important to take some time to identify individuals on whom you hope to make an impression through your direct and indirect impressions. Direct impressions include interactions with individuals who you see personally on a daily basis. For the purposes of this book, we will apply this concept to the professional field in which individuals are looking to advance their careers. In this instance, the direct impressions would occur with individuals such as classmates, colleagues, bosses, professors and/or upper-level leadership. These would be individuals who at some point may be in a position to help you advance by putting in a good word for you. If your direct impressions are strong enough, they may even go out of their way to help you get a job or a promotion. Indirect impressions include interactions that occur on a far less frequent basis, and often relate to the interactions that do not even happen in person. In today's technological environment, this can include digital contact with individuals and/or online materials which you put together to make an impression about the skill sets that you have to offer. Both direct and indirect impressions are keys to success in branding, and should be considered when developing a personal positioning strategy.

> ➤ Segmentation Implementation Step #1: With a computer or pad of paper, write down five individuals (or groups of individuals) who you would consider as critical for your future success. For now, limit this to five people so you can focus on strategic initiatives without getting overwhelmed. Once you have your list of five, move on to the next area of segmentation.

2. Considering the Interests of Key Segments

Once you have taken the time to prioritize your top target markets, there is another step you must take prior to developing your personal branding plan. While knowing who you will target in your efforts is important, it does little good if you do not take the time to understand the interests of the individuals whom you will be targeting. More importantly, you should think about the things that are important to them and then take it a step further by considering the ways that you could add value to them through your interactions and/or skill sets. As you go through this process, write things down so you can keep track of the areas that will be most important for maximizing efficiency in your efforts. By doing this, you can identify areas that overlap between the different target markets, and as a result you will start to prioritize the areas that you should focus on when developing your product.

> ➤ Segmentation Implementation Step #2: Using the target markets from the previous step, make a list of the things that each of these individuals/groups value (e.g., enhanced social media interaction). Another way to look at this is to focus on the areas in which you can add value to the individual. If this is difficult to do, you may need to take some time to identify these areas through feedback, evaluation, and/or formal research. Make sure you spend the time to do this because you do not want to waste energy on initiatives that are not effective.

3. Determining Strategies to Position Your Product

By spending time to find out what your key segments value, you provide yourself with information that is necessary for determining how you will proceed with personal branding initiatives. In essence, you have taken time to think about others and this step alone is something that will allow you to be far more effective in building relationships with others. With this structure in place, now is the time to decide how you can capitalize on the value areas so you are able to add value to others. Much of your success in this specific step will be determined by your ability to develop skills sets and/or behaviors that will enhance interactions with your key segments. During this process, be sure to only include strategies that you believe in, because they will come across as inauthentic if they are meaningless to you. At this point, you need to pursue being both authentic and realistic (based on time constraints) so you are identifying areas on which you can effectively follow through during the next 6 to 12 months.

> ➤ Segmentation Implementation Step #3: For each target market you have identified, rank their top three priority areas to which you believe you can add value. For each of these priority areas, strategically write down the steps you must take to accomplish adding value to the individual. At this point, it would be smart to consider both the things you need to do in the long-term (6-12 months) and on a daily basis to succeed.

> ➤ Segmentation Implementation Step #4: One strategy that is useful if you are feeling overwhelmed here is to make a comprehensive list of priority areas between your five different key target markets. Once you have combined them, you can keep track of the areas that seem to come up most often. With this strategy, you have the opportunity to identify five focus areas that will bring the largest return on investment for your time and energy for the cumulative list of your most important target markets.

SEGMENTATION IN ACTION

If you are anything like me, you need to be able to learn about things in a "hands on," practical situation to fully grasp marketing concepts. Regardless of whether the specific example is exactly the position you are in, the demonstration of the steps to a real situation will help you to apply things to your life. So, with this being said, it is time to get to work. For this example, we will focus on an individual college coach who is taking all the right steps to build his personal brand with key stakeholders surrounding his program.

Building Brand with Bono

Chris Bono is currently the head coach of the South Dakota State University (SDSU) wrestling program. When Coach Bono was first hired at this National Collegiate Athletic Association (NCAA) Division I wrestling program, he immediately made it a priority to invest in branding to build interest surrounding the program. You see, given the current landscape of college athletics, many smaller "Olympic" sport programs are limited on the support they receive and it is up to the coach to cultivate interest to grow the program. Given the competitive nature of Bono, he immediately took steps to develop a brand mantra for his program that his staff and athletes could rally around. However, for this brand to truly take hold, it was going to take modeling by a leader who could inspire energy surrounding the program. For the process to succeed, Coach Bono was going to have to build his personal brand with all the individuals surrounding his program so that he could realize his vision.

When a coach first steps into a role as a program leader, it is important to develop a culture that will guide stakeholders on a daily basis. If done properly, the values that are put into place for the program are extensions of the coach's philosophy because they are the ones who cast vision. For people to buy in to this process, they must believe in their leader and there is no way they will do this if the individual does not model the values they are attempting to implement. So, the first step for any person who is in a leadership position is to understand the values that matter most to them so they can model them daily to "followers." When organizational values matter deeply to a leader and the individual models them, there is a far greater chance they will get others to buy in to the organization's vision. In the process, they will also develop a brand that is authentic with the people who surround them.

Getting Started with Segmentation

For Coach Bono, one of the things that was critical when taking control of the program was to identify the individuals who will be most important to achieving success. From a program branding standpoint, there is no one that is more important to developing a culture than the staff and student-athletes. In essence, these are the individuals who will live the program values on a daily basis, and this essentially becomes a part of the daily interactions that people have with SDSU Wrestling. Thus, it makes sense that these two groups would be identified as primary target markets for Coach Bono to build his personal brand. On top of this, athletic administrators are certainly individuals who would be beneficial to have as supporters, as they would be considered superiors to most coaches. Finally, alumni are people who provide support to the program in terms of attending events and providing financial assistance, so they need to be added as a key target market as well. For efficiency purposes, we will limit the target markets to these four groups.

What You Value Is Not Necessarily What They Will Value

One of the easiest ways to fail in branding is to only consider things from your own perspective. Assuming that people all prefer the things you do is a mistake that will cost you when you are trying to build relationships with people who are key to success in your life. So, now that we have identified the individuals who matter most to Coach Bono, it makes sense to take the time to think about ways for him to build his personal brand with these groups of people. In order to do this, we need to take the second step in segmentation and consider the things that matter most to each of the key target markets. In the section below, we have broken down the basic description of the group along with the specific interests that are unique to each segment. Once we have provided this background, we will move on to the creative strategies that could be implemented to add value to people. This will allow us to tie the concepts back to personal branding for you regardless of the situation that you are coming from.

1. Coaching Staff. The coaching staff members consist of assistant coaches who are a key part of success because they help coordinate all aspects of the program. In addition, they are an extremely visible part of the program because they interact with all other key stakeholders that are essential to efficient brand building.

➤ Primary Interests: (1) Advancement in coaching career, (2) ability to contribute to program, and (3) personal recognition.

2. Student-Athletes. Student-athletes are potentially the most important target market for coaches because they are the individuals who compete for the team. On top of this, their actions both during competitions and social situations determine the overall brand for the team.

➤ Primary Interests: (1) Ability to realize athletic goals, (2) opportunity for career after graduation, and (3) personal recognition.

3. Administrators. The leaders in college athletic departments who are assigned with the task of ensuring they are putting resources in position to help department realize goals. These also happen to be the individuals who make the decision on the level of support that programs receive in the department.

➤ Primary Interests: (1) Ability to realize department expectations, (2) opportunity to advance career, (3) personal recognition.

4. Alumni. The alumni are individuals who graduated from the program and have a vested stake in making sure the program succeeds. Because of this, these are individuals who are likely to provide support to the program in terms of attending events and providing financial assistance.

➤ Primary Interests: (1) Helping the program advance, (2) being connected to the program, (3) personal recognition.

BEING CREATIVE WITH WAYS TO ADD VALUE TO PEOPLE.

All people enjoy it when critical individuals in their life see the things they are doing as valuable. The interesting thing is that few people develop the ability to see things from these people's perspectives. Whether you like it or not, you sometimes have to go out of your way to add value to people if you would like them to take the time to see things from your perspective (and to help you out). By taking the time to understand the primary interests of key target markets, we now know the areas in which we can add value to others, and as a result we can make daily decisions that will build our personal brand with them. If we want to cultivate a unique relationship with our assistants, then we need to invest in them daily so that they are able to advance their careers. By doing this, you will build your relationship with them and they will be far more likely to help you achieve your vision. In the process, you will also indirectly build a reputation for adding value to others and as a result they will often tell others about you. Similarly, when attempting to build your brand with the other target markets, you can go out of your way to develop strategies to publicly recognize them for their contributions to the program and to your success. Doing this in a selfless manner will build loyalty with others and this will eventually become a part of your reputation. The key in this process is to identify ways in which you can add value to key people in your life on a daily basis.

TAKE HOME POINT—
PURSUE CONSISTENT POSITIVE INTERACTIONS

The one way to ensure you are always building a positive brand is by trying to make a positive impression on everyone that you meet. When you learn to value people and all individual interactions, you maximize the chances of building a positive relationship with people who have the potential to advance your career and your life. In addition to this being the right approach for efficiency in branding, you absolutely never know when you will interact with an individual who has the ability to influence your life. By making positive impressions as often as possible, you maximize the chances that you will have people that will vouch for you as a person and/

or as a professional. With this being said, it certainly makes sense to target certain individuals who are important to your career and life progression. While you should make it a habit to treat all people well, these are individuals who you can identify so you are able to develop a product and an approach that will impress them. The key here is to make sure that you take into consideration other people's interests so you are able to make decisions that will add value to them in some unique way.

IMPRESSIONS IMPLEMENTATION EXERCISE

Based on the segmentation implementation steps that you took in the chapter, you now know some of the individuals you will target in your personal branding efforts.

1. With your five top priority areas, identify at least one specific strategy that you can put into place to make sure that you are adding value to key target markets. If there are certain ones that are more prevalent than others across segments, you may want to prioritize them and make sure they are the first that you implement.

CHAPTER 9

Cultivate a Care Mindset for People

～

"To add value to others, one must first value others."

—*John C. Maxwell*

Personal branding is a concept that deals largely with positioning yourself for other people. Similar to successful
marketing endeavors in general, it is near impossible to
be successful in branding if you do not care about people. Simply
put, when you care about them, you are far more likely to consider
their perceptions and make decisions that will position you more
effectively for key target markets. On top of this, the concept of
considering others makes you think more specifically about the
skill sets you need to develop to make your product unique. There
are not many things more important than learning to value other
people when attempting to build a unique personal brand. It is a
step that is essential to success in branding so we will spend some
time discussing it in-depth during this chapter.

WHAT PERSONAL BRANDING IS NOT . . .

Personal branding is not a gimmick. While some people see it as a quick way to make a superficial impression to gain an advantage, the truth is that it is about living a solid lifestyle in which you are proactive about building sound relationships. It is not a way to cut corners so you can get the things that you want out of life. Instead, it involves learning to put other people's interests first so that you can add value to their lives. It is not about making decisions so you can be perceived as extremely important and above other people. Instead, as you already likely know, personal branding is about learning to live the right way so you can work well with other people. And when you make sound decisions and live daily by the right values, it is likely that you will end up being able to achieve all of the elements of your vision. As explained by leadership teacher legend Zig Ziglar, "You will get all the things that you want in life if you help enough other people get what they want."

YOU CANNOT FAKE AUTHENTICITY

We have already established the importance of authenticity when interacting with people around you. There is no question that you can trick some people in the short run by telling them what they want to hear. However, if you are around people for an extended period of time, they will eventually see that your actions are not aligning with what you are saying. When this happens, it will hurt your authenticity and you will eventually struggle to build credibility in relationships. The only way to build credibility with people is to treat them the right way in your interactions. Make it a priority to follow through on the things that you say you will and do whatever you can to add value to people's lives. However, be aware that you cannot fake caring about people in the long run. You must truly value them or it will eventually show in your actions.

In leadership guru Dr. John Maxwell's "Establishing Credibility" podcast he talks about developing the ability to build credibility with people around you.[1] One of the things that Dr. Maxwell explains is that it is easy to fool people with your words when you are first around people. In essence, they will take you at your word early on in a relationship because they have not had a chance to see you in action. However, he explains that eventually your actions will become more important than your words and people will assess the type of person you are by the things you do on a daily basis. At this point, you will no longer be able to fool the people around you because they will know who you are. This is why it is so important to make sure that you are modeling the things that matter most to you. Eventually, this is how people will see us and this will become our brand.

MAKE A COMMITMENT TO CARE

One of the best ways to build a personal brand that is positive with others is to truly care about them. When you make a commitment to valuing people, you will naturally see their interests and will be far more likely to make decisions that will build your reputation with them. Have you ever had a coach or teacher that truly cared about you? I bet you can remember that it never seemed to be about them and they were always trying to do things to help you realize your full potential and goals. As a result, they were able to get the most out of you and you will probably always remember them for that. One of the primary reasons why they were able to build this relationship with you is because they truly cared about you and it was an authentic approach. Because they likely did this with a variety of people in their lives, they were the type of individual in whom people believed and wanted to be around. Their ability to add value to others created a positive personal brand with a wide range of people, and this likely opened up opportunities in their life. While there are a variety of factors at play here, the core foundational element was a commitment to care about people.

CULTIVATING CARE CAN TAKE TIME

In theory, caring about other people seems like a fairly straightforward concept. And it is one most of us can willingly admit as being an important commitment for succeeding in our life. However, the follow through can be very difficult because we all have some selfish habits that we have developed at different points in our lives. Aside from this, it is also natural to be driven to want to achieve great things from a personal standpoint. It is important to understand that it is these habits that will prevent us from being able to truly show care for other people. If your drive to realize personal recognition is greater than the drive to add value to others, this will eventually show through your actions and people may be hesitant to support your vision. With this being the case, commit to caring about people and strive to put them first in your interactions. Be cognizant of the fact that it may take time to eliminate selfish habits that you have formed over the years. If you are aware of your actions and are persistent to show you care about people, you will eventually build a personal brand that is unique to all of the people who are fortunate enough to interact with you. There is a reason very few people are able to accomplish being like your old coach or teacher. It is extremely difficult to learn to put other people first. I am still battling to make this happen every single day and there are old habits that reemerge when I am not disciplined with my approach. This is when I remind myself that the process of cultivating a care mindset takes time.

SAYING AND DOING ARE TWO DIFFERENT THINGS

We have all met people that talk about how selfless they are and how other people are their first priorities. Then they do things that make you realize that they are only worried about themselves. There are two lessons to learn from these people. First, the incongruences between their actions and words often put a strain on their relationships and hurt their personal brand with others. Second, especially with the most well-intentioned people, you realize that it is very difficult to follow through on your intentions in life. The take home point here is that saying and doing are two completely different things. While saying you care about people is great, it means nothing if you do not learn to follow through and show it with your actions. You know you are really on the right track when there are times when you put your own needs on the backburner to do something for someone else. While it is certainly not possible to do this all the time, you should strive to have the balance tip in favor of doing things for others. The higher the percentage of doing things for others, the higher the chance that you will build a personal brand that shows a genuine care for others.

WHY DOES CARING MATTER IN BRANDING

We have already established that effective personal branding is largely influenced by the ability to consider the interests of the people who are essential to success in our lives. In essence, if we want to build a personal brand that is positive with people, we need to learn to position ourselves in a manner that will be valuable to others. Caring about others is a big step in making sure that you will open your mind enough to see what is most valuable to them. If you are faking it, there is a good chance that you will take a shortcut that will end up backfiring on you in the long run. Furthermore, because branding is about negative and positive interactions, the ability to care helps ensure that you will be far more likely to have significantly more positive interactions with people. And when this occurs, the likelihood of you having a unique personal brand is far greater as well. On top of this, the caring aspect will cultivate a loyalty with people that will bring more flexibility when you make mistakes. And finally, because we are all driven in some way by personal achievements, you will increase your chances of success by caring about the people around you. If you are able to show that you care about people, they will be far more likely to get on board to support your vision. This alone is enough to want caring to be a part of your personal brand.

DO ENOUGH FOR OTHERS AND THEY WILL EVENTUALLY DO FOR YOU

Most people would like others to see their perspectives and to do things for them. The trouble is that many people are wired this way and you must first step up and do something for others before they are willing to help you. You absolutely want to make caring a part of your brand because it is necessary for achieving the goals that you have in your life. You must be the one to initiate this process and you should do it with no expectations for what you will get in return. The goal should simply be to become an individual who is able to connect with people so you are seen as a positive person. These are the exact interactions that will build your brand, and eventually you will realize the benefits that come from being a caring person. As leadership guru John Maxwell explained, "People don't care how much you know until they know how much you care." To help illustrate this point, we will discuss two companies that have moved to legendary branding status by making "caring about people" a central part of their brand.

DELIVERING HAPPINESS:
THE ZAPPOS WOW SERVICE PHILOSOPHY

Founded in 1999 as an online shoe store, Zappos is now an online retailer that does over $1 billion in revenue each year. In addition, they were named as the highest-ranking newcomer in Fortune magazine's annual "Best Companies to Work For" list in 2009.[2] While they have created a unique culture featuring 10 unique core values, at the center of their success is their "Deliver WOW Through Service" philosophy. This has not been something that has just been for show though. They have modeled this value by making sure they hire people that embrace their philosophy. In fact, they actually offer brand-new employees $2000 to quit following an initial training period to make sure they get committed team members. In addition, they ensure that employees embrace this philosophy by treating their staff extremely well on a daily basis. As a result, their employees have been known to go out of their way to over deliver for customers on a regular basis. The stories that circulate about their organization have become legendary online and their word-of-mouth advertising has become essential to their success. While not one of the more flashy stories, they will often add complementary two-day shipping for customers just to add value to their experience. How is this for modeling care through their actions? The end result is that their brand is now known for being one of the best customer service organizations in the retail business. Their approach is now an example for organizations looking to develop a unique culture that adds value to employees and customers.

SOUTHWEST AIRLINES' SECRET TO SUCCESS: DO THE RIGHT THING

Southwest Airlines is an example of another organization that has done something truly amazing in the business world. Moving into an extremely competitive industry with high barriers to entry, they have been able to become one of the premier airlines because of their philosophy to put people first before their profits.[3] Their "Southwest Cares" mantra has truly become a part of their brand as their customers tend to see them as an airline that takes the time to show courtesy and a little creativity. In addition to caring, they have become known for the attendants who strive to make a customer's experience unique during their flight. One example of this is an attendant who actually engages the passengers in an interactive demonstration as he raps the safety demo prior to leaving the gate.[4] Southwest has encouraged creativity and this has cultivated innovative interactions with customers that make their experience unique while flying with the airline. The end result is that people have a loyal connection with the airline because they know Southwest cares about them as a customer. The creativity just reinforces this in the organization's brand and tends to add a little entertainment value that people remember as well.

COYTE G. COOPER, PH.D.

Do What Southwest and Zappos Does . . .

I know what you are thinking. What do billion dollar companies have to do with my personal brand? They actually have a lot more in common with you than you think when it comes to branding. As we have learned, the process of branding has to do with the ability to identify and model values on a daily basis. When these interactions are consistent, eventually you will have an opportunity to realize your brand vision. This is exactly what these organizations have done on a much larger scale. They took the time to know what they wanted to be and made sure that their values reflected this. Then they went about developing a culture that embraced these values, starting from the top. Eventually, their employees bought in to the philosophy and now consistently model these values to customers on a regular basis. The good news for you is that you only have to worry about one person modeling the values that are most important to build your personal brand. If you have the self-discipline these organizations have demonstrated over time, then you will also have an opportunity to develop a brand that adds value to the people around you. The outcome will also be the same with loyal followers who will say good things about you to the people that they know. This is called word-of-mouth advertising and it is exactly the type of benefit that you want to realize when investing in personal branding.

Care Does Not Mean You Are Weak

I know what some of you are thinking. If you make caring a part of your brand, then other people will think you are weak. Do not confuse kindness with being soft on people. The reality is that you can care about people and still hold them to a high standard. In fact, this is sometimes the best way to get them to pursue a higher standard because they will be more likely to listen to you when they know you care. If you are in a leadership position, the key here is to make sure that your kindness comes with expectations that people must meet. And when they fall short, there are consequences they must live by. You can do this while also having their best interests in mind. Even if you are not in a leadership position, it is very important to show your care for people while being willing to stand up for yourself and for what you believe in. The ability to protect your values is something that most people will respect when you approach things the right way. And when they don't, you can live with it because you will be modeling your values and doing things the way you know you should.

TAKE HOME POINT— BEING REAL BUILDS RELATIONSHIPS

One of the most important components in branding is authenticity. You are better off consistently being something less than ideal than occasionally being something that you are not. Let me put it another way. People will be far more accepting of you modeling marginal values than if you are inconsistent with exceptional values. In our society, it has become a trend for individuals to pretend to be something they are not in order to impress the people around them. I am sure that many of you have been around these types of people. In these instances, the individuals around them often resent them and tend to think that the people are fake. This is absolutely not something you want if you are trying to build relationships that will enhance your life. Building on authenticity, there is extreme value in considering caring as one of your values if you want to succeed in connecting with people. By putting other people first in a meaningful way, you are well on your way to living an extraordinary life and building an extraordinary personal brand.

IMPRESSIONS IMPLEMENTATION EXERCISE

Based on what you learned during this chapter, answer each of the questions below. This will help guide you as we move to being great at individual interactions in the next chapter.

1. In the past, what are the situations that may have caused you to come across as inauthentic to the people around you? In addition to identifying these here now, pay attention to your actions during the next week to see if anything surfaces. It is important that you keep an open mind or you will not see these areas.

2. What are the specific ways that you can show the key people around you that you care about them? Identify how important it is to you at this point to embrace these strategies in your life.

3. Are there areas in which kindness could justifiably be seen as weakness? If so, how will you make sure that you are being kind while holding high expectations at the same time?

CHAPTER 10

Insist on Being Extraordinary at Individual Interactions

⤞⤝

"It's the little details that are vital. Little things make big things happen."

—*John Wooden*

One of the most challenging concepts to embrace in personal branding is the ability to capitalize on individual interactions. You could argue this would be the case for meaningful success in any area of life. I am sure you have heard the saying, "If it was easy, everybody would do it." Well, this is certainly true in modeling your values, living well, and building a unique personal brand. The truth is that branding is made up of a collection of individual interactions that you have on a daily basis. Most people can make the right decision one time or when it is easy to do so. The most successful people are the ones that learn to make the right decisions all the time, including when life presents its regular challenges. When you are dragging in the morning and don't feel like getting your day started, you need to get your mind right and focus on all the opportunities being presented around you. There are interactions happening all around us throughout the day and we cannot afford to miss out on opportunities to build our reputation. When we understand the importance of individual interactions, we have taken the first step necessary to realize our full potential. It is at this point we can start to value interactions in a way that we will always be putting our best foot forward. This chapter will be dedicated to helping you succeed in this area.

ONE OF THE GREATEST OF ALL-TIME AT INDIVIDUAL INTERACTIONS

Many of you are probably familiar with the name John Wooden. This is because he is known as one of the greatest coaches in the history of college sports. Wooden, a legendary coach at UCLA, won 10 NCAA Championships (7 in a row) and set a record for most consecutive games won (88 straight).[1] While his accomplishments are extraordinary, what is even more impressive about Coach Wooden is the way he approached coaching the game of basketball. His attention to detail is well documented as he did everything possible to make sure his players embraced the little details during practice and competition. It was not uncommon for Coach Wooden to spend time teaching his players how to tie their shoes properly because he believed it would minimize injury and save time in practices. He was the master of paying attention to the little things and as a result his accomplishments ended up being truly unique. This concept is something that is no different for individuals looking to accomplish great things in personal branding efforts. You must develop the ability to embrace seemingly insignificant, "smaller" interactions if you want to make a lasting impression on others around you.

What Exactly Are Individual Interactions?

You may still be asking yourself exactly what individual interactions are. While we have referenced this concept throughout the book, there has not been a specific in-depth description provided to outline its implications. From a personal branding standpoint, this involves any interaction that we have with people on a daily basis. When you correspond with people in a casual manner, you are interacting with them and almost always have the opportunity to make some kind of impression on them. If you are working with colleagues or co-workers in a work setting, you are constantly in contact with them and the quality of your actions will determine how they see you over time. It is important to recognize a couple of things at this point. First, the success of your individual interactions has to do with both how you treat people and your ability to be productive (personally and as a leader helping others). Second, the ability to capitalize on individual interactions only realizes full potential when you do it consistently over time. Being great at individual interactions sporadically will not do you any good. In fact, it can even come across as inauthentic if you are inconsistent with your efforts. You absolutely must learn to be a master of consistency if you are going to reach full potential in branding and leadership.

Laying the Groundwork for "Instinctual Interactions"

The good news at this point in the book is that you already have the tools necessary to become more "instinctual" in positive individual interactions. If you have chosen the right values, you will naturally already have a start to making this happen because they will guide you in the right direction each day. If you have started to model them consistently, then some of your interactions are going to start to become more natural because they are an extension of who you are. One of the keys here is making sure that you are constantly learning about your values and how you can improve your performance in each area. By becoming a lifelong learner in these areas, you ensure that you are constantly striving to improve who you are and how you are interacting with people. The framework for being great at individual interactions is growing yourself on a daily basis. When you develop your mind consistently, you will always have the opportunity to improve what you have to offer to people around you. Equally important, the consistent repetition in value areas will strengthen your mental muscles and they will become more instinctual in nature.

FIND A WAY TO FOCUS ON THE PRESENT

Another tip to make sure you are great at individual interactions is developing the ability to live in the moment. If we are not aware of our approach, we can often get too caught up in the past and the future. When we make mistakes, there is a strong urge to overanalyze and/or dwell on them. It is important we do not do this because it costs us our ability to live in the present as we interact with the people around us. Similarly, spending too much time thinking of the future robs us of being able to capitalize on opportunities to connect with people and make a lasting impression on them. To ensure that you are always making the most of your actions, you must focus sharply on being present in each moment of the day. While there are certainly times for reflection and setting vision, most of your day should be dedicated to living your values to the best of your ability. Be patient with yourself because you will have to cultivate the ability to block out distractions and focus on the areas that are most important to you. This is often challenging because it involves overcoming bad habits that you developed over time.

LEARNING TO LISTEN INTENTLY

We already know how important it is to value people when striving to build a unique brand that leaves a lasting impression. One of the best ways to show people that you value them is by listening to them when they are talking. While this sounds like a simple concept, it is actually very difficult to accomplish. I have to admit that it is something that I continue to battle because my natural tendency is to want to form a response when people are talking. The problem here is that it is impossible to actually hear what people are saying when you are forming a response and worrying solely about getting your opinion across. As you approach each day, be aware of when you are doing this and make a commitment to stop and truly listen to people. When you take the time to listen, you will eventually hear things that will allow you to build your relationship with people. As we have discussed, a major part of branding is adding value to others and you cannot do this if you do not know what other people value.

Another thing to realize is it is often pretty easy to listen to someone when you need something immediate from them. In these instances, you know something is at stake so it is easy to stay engaged long enough to communicate what it is you need from them. Even in these situations, be sure to remind yourself that the purpose of communication (and branding) should not solely be about getting what you need from others. While the selfish approach can sometimes work in the short term, it will eventually backfire because people will realize that you do not care about them. This is a primary reason why you need to make communication a priority before you actually need something from someone. When you do this, it will often show people that you care about them and they will be far more likely to respond when you actually do need something important from them.

BE IN THE BUSINESS OF READING BODY LANGUAGE

Given that the foundation of personal branding is adding value to others, it is essential you place a priority on communication. We have already discussed the importance of learning to listen to others around you on a consistent basis. However, this is not the only thing you need to do if you are going to become effective at connecting with people. Many times, there is much more to a conversation than what a person is telling you. If you pay close attention, you will quickly realize that body language can tell you a lot about a person. While they may be saying they are all right with you taking over their work assignment, their lack of eye contact and flaring of the nostrils can tell you otherwise. While most situations won't deal with something quite this obvious, the point is you can learn a lot about what matters most to a person by observing their body's responses during interactions about key topic areas. The ability to read others and the environment in a room will go a long way in making sure you are making decisions that will build relationships with others.

THE MENTALITY OF MAKING AN IMPRESSION

You could take all of the previous steps in this book and fail at developing a unique personal brand if you do not care about making a lasting impression on others. You will not realize your full potential with people if you are not fully committed to making the most of interactions on a daily basis. "Make a Habit of Making Extraordinary Impressions" should be one of your central values that you wake up and remind yourself of first thing in the morning. Whether this relates to your kids, spouse, colleague, friend, or future employer (depending on key target markets), it should be one of your passions to make decisions that will add value to their lives daily. You should consider the ways you can maximize interactions with them and visualize yourself making these things happen consistently. The ability to embrace this mindset will go a long way in ensuring that you are enhancing relationships with the people around you that matter most. When you do this consistently with no expectations for what you will get in return, there is a good chance that you will have lots of good fortune in your life.

The Value of Visualization in Branding

We have already touched on a form of visualization when we went through the steps of developing a brand vision for our life. In essence, this is the visualization process that focuses on our long-term aspirations that will guide our decisions on a daily basis. While this is a critical step to success in personal branding and leadership, there is another form of visualization that we need to embrace if we are going to succeed at making a lasting impression on the people around us. Once you know the values that matter most to you, it is important that you take the time to visualize yourself living these values as you interact with people. While this may seem strange, understand that repetition is one of the most important elements of making sure you are living your values as best as possible. When you see them in your head, it is like a repetition that goes towards your mastery of modeling the areas that are most important to you. If it works well for elite athletes, there is no reason why we cannot apply this to other areas of life in which we are looking to perform at a high level. When you wake up each morning, take the time to see yourself living each day as well as possible as you model your core values during normal interactions.

MAKE EACH DAY A MASTERPIECE

As we have discussed in this chapter, one of the first steps to building a unique brand that will be recognized by others is to master the application of the fundamentals during each interaction with people. Once you have grasped this concept and know you can control individual interactions, the goal should be for you to make each day a masterpiece. Take pride in knowing you have done everything in your power to model values and to maximize relationships in your life. If you get in the habit of making each day a masterpiece, eventually this will become who you are and you will develop an amazing personal brand that influences the people around you a great deal. It is important to remind yourself that this process starts with a simple commitment to make the most of singular interactions that you have with singular individuals. You have to take care of little things before you are able to accomplish big things.

YOU NEVER KNOW WHEN YOU WILL MAKE A DIFFERENCE

The focus of this book is learning to live life extremely well so you can ensure you are developing a personal brand that opens up opportunities in your life. It is probably clear at this point that you need to be able to add value to others if you want to build strong relationships that will bring benefits to your life in the long run. My hope is that you are passionate about working to add value to the people around you because it is the right thing to do. When this becomes a part of who you are, there is a good chance that something truly special will happen to you. As you invest in the people around you, there will come a moment in which you realize that you have changed someone's life for the better. When this moment comes, I believe that you will truly see that this is one of the most rewarding outcomes that life has to offer. This is the time in which you will commit to having "making a difference" as one of the central values in your life. Interestingly, this is also a value that can bring amazing benefits to your life when it is done with a selfless approach.

TAKE HOME POINT—
EMBRACE INDIVIDUAL OPPORTUNITIES TO IMPRESS

If you are going to reach full potential in personal branding and life, you need to become great at taking control of individual interactions. As we move through each day, there are literally hundreds of opportunities to make impressions on others that eventually add up to make our brand unique. While you may not be able to control every single interaction, you can certainly get in the habit of consciously placing real value on the ones with key people in our lives. If we are modeling the right types of core values, there is a good chance that we will make solid impressions on the remaining interactions. One of the keys in this area is learning to take the time to listen and to watch the people around us so we can learn the things that are most important to them. When we have this information, we can start to make decisions that will allow us to better connect with people on a daily basis. Eventually, constant progress in this area will allow you to build a unique personal brand while changing people's lives around you.

IMPRESSIONS IMPLEMENTATION EXERCISE

It is critical that you learn to focus on the present if you are going to succeed in personal branding. One way to ensure you are doing this is by taking time each morning to get your mind in the right place to approach the day. To help with this, be sure to give yourself 15-30 minutes (depending on your schedule) each morning to focus on the following items.

1. For the first 5-10 minutes, focus on all the things that you are grateful for in your life. When you first start this, you may need to make a list of these items so you can revisit them on a regular basis. By focusing on your areas of gratitude, you train your mind to find the positive and this will ultimately become a part of your brand.

2. For the second 5-10 minutes, focus on the vision you have identified and picture yourself achieving it in your mind. The power of clarity will help you to believe you are fully capable of realizing your dreams. This is a critical element to eventually realizing your vision.

3. For the third 10 minutes, revisit each of the values that will be essential for you to realize full potential and your brand vision. In addition, consider the ways that you will model them within your daily schedule.

If you are going to be extremely efficient in your personal branding efforts, you must learn to train your mind to focus sharply on your vision, values, and daily approach. By making a habit of envisioning key elements on a daily basis, you create a structure that increases the chance of success moving forward.

PHASE 3

Creative Approaches to Differentiate Your Brand

Follow-Through

CHAPTER 11

Capitalize on Key Brand
Interaction Spots

❧

*"How can you squander even one more day not taking
advantage of the greatest shifts of our generation? How dare
you settle for less when the world has made it so easy for you
to be remarkable?"*

—Seth Godin

We have spent a significant amount of time in this book discussing the importance of making an impression by taking control of individual interactions. The primary focus up to this point has been on personal interactions due to the fact that face-to-face dialogue is often the primary way we build relationships with people. However, it is important to note that technology has drastically changed the way we interact with people on a daily basis. On both a personal and professional level, many of us use technology as a regular form of communication to connect and stay in touch with key people in our lives. While there is a wide range of mediums that we use on a regular basis, we will narrow in on a few key areas in this chapter to help hit home on key personal branding points. The good news is the areas we will cover are concepts that will apply to any other technological medium that you choose to use to interact with people. For now, we will start with an area that seems to be on everyone's mind these days because of the popularity of social media. Given that billions of people currently engage in social media usage, it makes sense to start with how you can leverage these platforms to build your brand the right way.

THE SALIENCE OF SOCIAL MEDIA

When talking about personal branding, social media is almost always one of the most popular areas that people want to discuss. This makes sense when you think about it, given that there are so many people interacting on social media outlets on a daily basis. At the moment, the top three social media sites (Facebook, Twitter, and LinkedIn) all have over 250 million active monthly users.[1] Whether you like it or not, social media has become a part of the communication culture in today's society. However, this does not mean that people know what they are doing or that they are making decisions that provide them with the best opportunity to succeed in the future. Instead, you could argue that many people are making decisions on social media on a daily basis that will cost them opportunities in their life. This is exactly why it is so important that we discuss social media in this chapter. When used properly, social media can be something that helps you cultivate connections and build relationships with people that can help you to advance in life. It is necessary to understand this will not happen if you do not know how to use it in a manner that will build your brand.

SOCIAL MEDIA BRANDING 101

If you are interested in building your personal brand and are involved in social media, you should consider all of the previous areas we have discussed in this book prior to posting. While in electronic format, your interactions very much matter in the same way they do in face-to-face interactions because your dialogue will determine what people think of you. Every time you post something, people take it in and intuitively make an assessment about the type of person that you are. If you are posting positive things that add value to people's lives, you are likely to gain followers and people are more likely to associate good things with your name. On the flip side, when you are posting negative things and creating conflict, people will likely associate negative things with your name and this will eventually hurt your brand. This is assuming that you are interested in building a productive, meaningful reputation. On top of this, be sure to consider the fact that social media has a compounding factor due to the fact that people can, and often do, share your messages. Quality posts have the potential to spread to additional people that could become connections and bad messages have the potential to spread to additional people that may not want to associate with you. It is always important to remind yourself that you often attract what you are putting out to the world through your interactions.

IMPLICATIONS OF IRRESPONSIBLE POSTS

One of the biggest mistakes people make on social media is posting irresponsible content to which they give very little thought. I have come to the conclusion that these are individuals who do not have a thorough understanding of personal branding. Rather, they post without a plan and rarely take the time to think about how their actions will influence the perceptions others have about them. The good news here is you can make a change with a simple adjustment to your mindset and approach. Similar to the concepts we have discussed earlier in this book, you simply need to take the time to think about how you want people to see you on social media and then consider how each of your posts will impact it. If you want to open up meaningful opportunities for yourself in the future, make the decision right now to avoid posts that will detract from building a differentiated brand that is conducive to success.

RULES FOR "REPUTATION BUILDING" BRANDING

Whether you are experienced or not in social media, you need to develop some rules that will guide your actions when using sites such as Facebook, Instagram, and Twitter. If you are going to be in the business of personal branding, you would be wise to accept the fact that all of your posts matter. Now that you understand the concept of branding, it should be much easier for you to stop and assess whether or not you should follow through on specific posts. As you move forward, consider exactly what you would like to achieve via social media and make sure your posts are conducive for your vision in this area. I can tell you with full confidence that your brand on social media should be guided by the values you have created earlier in this book. In the meantime, I have developed some basic rules you should always follow when you are using social media. It doesn't matter who you are, these are concepts that can help you make sure you are building a positive reputation with others.

Rule #1:
Be in the Biz of Branding

If you have made it to this point in the book, there is no question that you are interested in building a unique personal brand that opens up opportunities in your life. Given this is the case, your interactions on social media should simply be an extension of who you are. Whenever you are considering a post on social media, it makes sense to stop and ask yourself whether or not it will help or hurt your personal brand. If it hurts your brand, then you need to consider the implications and move on to something else that is more productive. While this will seem robotic at the start, eventually you will get a good feel for your brand and will not need to stop and remind yourself to do this. However, you should always be in the business of branding if you want to make a positive impression on the people who see your messages on social media.

Rule #2:
Know There's No Privacy

I am always amazed at the types of things that people are willing to post on social media. It is as if they have no grasp of the fact that people are actually following the posts they are releasing. It doesn't seem to even matter if they are following other people and making judgments about their messages because they lack the mindset necessary for self-reflection. On a basic level, you need to understand that there are people paying attention to the things you are posting. Second, as we touched on in the previous rule, there is a potential for your messages to circulate and reach additional people you had no intention of it reaching. So, if you are going to write comments blasting a teacher about a class, remind yourself that there are people who will share this and it might get back to the teacher that you are writing about. Third, even if you have privacy settings in place, the people who have permission to follow you can find a way to capture your posts and share them with others. The bottom line is there is no privacy in social media and everything you post counts towards your reputation. Once you fully grasp this concept, you can move on to being proactive about posting things that will ensure you have a positive brand image.

Rule #3:
Practice the Golden Rule

One of the things that makes social media so cool is it allows people to interact with each other in a creative manner. The platforms of top sites allow users to post content and create dialogue in a way that engages people. However, it doesn't take long while using social media to see there is a downside to these capabilities. For some reason, there are a lot of people that enjoy writing negative things about others. While this often gets attention and "shares," you should never engage in this behavior because it sends the wrong message about the type of person you are. And if you don't think this matters, then just search for individuals who have put their lives and career in serious danger because of the poor decisions they have made while using social media. To avoid this situation, make a commitment to practice the Golden Rule when posting on social media sites. While nice is sometimes not the most popular route, it will always pay the biggest dividends down the road when it comes to developing a unique personal brand that involves strong relationships with people.

Rule #4:
Think Twice for RT's

Another interesting thing I have observed is that people do not tend to think about the implications for the things they retweet (RT) or share. The fact that you did not create the content does not mean you can post it and have no branding implications. Whenever you RT or share a message, it is as if you are at least putting a small level of approval on the content that is being featured. You can be sure that people will judge you for the things you are sharing from others so think twice the next time you RT something that is negative in nature.

Rule #5:
Take a 'Cool Off' Period

If you spend enough time on social media, it is inevitable that somebody will say something that will get under your skin. It may be something directed at you or directed at someone else, but the end result will be that you want to respond and confront the individual. When this time comes, DO NOT write anything!!! If you do, there is a strong likelihood you will write something you might regret because you are responding with the emotional part of your brain. Instead, walk away from your electronic device and take a 20-30 minute cool off period. When you do this, you will give the logical part of your brain time to catch up so you can write something that is both reasonable and conducive to a productive brand. My guess is that anybody who reads this book can think of a time when they responded immediately with emotion and said something they regretted. If this is the case, then this is a concept that will truly resonate with you. So, the next time you are on social media and someone tweets something at you that gets you fired up, take a break and spend some time thinking about what is the most intelligent way to respond. While this may take longer when you first start to implement the concept, eventually this will become much shorter because you will naturally know how you want to respond based on experience.

Rule #6:
Cut Out the Controversy

Make a decision right now if you want your brand to be positive or negative on social media. If positive is the decision you made, then commit today to cutting out the controversy from your posts. I'm sure all of you who use social media can think of individuals who get into confrontational exchanges on a regular basis. Again, similar to what we talked about in the "Think Twice for RTs," it is as if people do not understand that other people can see the things that they are writing. While some people might find negative posts as entertaining, the larger majority would likely prefer that you not air your dirty laundry on their feed. And if you have lofty goals for your career and life, you can be sure that some of your key target markets will not find this as something that is useful. After all, who really wants to hire someone who is constantly getting into controversial situations on social media? Make a commitment to writing things that are positive in nature and add value to your followers.

Rule #7:
Build Your Network

If you are going to maximize your potential when using social media, you need to be intentional about your approach. Given the prevalence of sites such as Facebook, Instagram, and Twitter in today's society, there is a good chance that some of your key target markets engage in social media use. With this being the case, be on the look out for opportunities to connect with people that you see as a valuable asset to your career and/or life. Once you know who these individuals are, follow them on social media so you can see exactly what they are posting. If they have a regular presence, you can gauge the things they post to learn about what they value. On top of this, take the opportunity to strategically interact with them so you can get on their radar. Keep in mind that most active social media users appreciate it when you post nice things about them because it enhances their reputation. While it is certainly true that more in-depth interactions will likely occur via email or phone, there may be an opportunity to make initial contact via social media. In addition, when you meet people in a more informal manner (e.g., guest talks, casual introductions), social media sites such as Twitter can be an ideal way to encourage future conversations. Be sure to constantly look for ways you can build your network using technology. As quoted at the start of the chapter, iconic marketer Seth Godin asks, how dare you settle for anything less when the world (social media) has made it so easy for you to be spectacular?

ELECTRONIC INTERACTION

Another form of interaction that takes place regularly via technology is email. While it seems to be less of a priority for younger generations, it will absolutely play a critical role for electronic dialogue in the immediate future because of its prevalence in today's society. Similar to all of the other areas in this book, the problem here is that people rarely take the time to think about how their email exchanges will influence the way people think about them. In particular with younger generations, I am not sure they comprehend that their lack of attention to a prompt response and proper grammar have a direct influence on the way their professor, employer, and/or future employer perceive them. It is the attention to the little details like this that will allow you to make a positive impression on others.

Avoid the Clutter

There is a strange theme that has slowly emerged in our society. We are at a point where we are more connected than ever and yet the ability to communicate effectively seems to be getting worse for some people. I attribute this to the clutter that comes with having so much at our fingertips with our smart phones. There are so many ways to interact, entertain, and consume that we can easily become distracted from some of the things that are most important to our success. It is so important that you do not allow this to happen if you want to build productive relationships with people who can help you advance in your life. Whenever you receive emails from individuals you are looking to make an impression on, you should respond immediately if at all possible. And if not, you should find a way to remind yourself so you respond at your earliest convenience. When you do not, you risk the chance of forgetting to respond at all because of the clutter that we previously discussed. This is exactly the type of thing that will make people think you are irresponsible and/or lazy. By taking small steps to prevent this, you can minimize the temptations that arise from clutter and increase the chances that you will follow through on your intentions.

Pay Attention to the Little Things

With the format of social media, there is a premium placed on brevity in messaging. This is even the case if it comes at the cost of proper grammar and etiquette. In fact, many sites like Twitter encourage this due to the fact that you are limited to 140 characters and the culture rewards unique approaches. While there is nothing wrong with this, it is important you consider the individuals you are corresponding with when using email. If social media is a culture to which you are willing to adapt, then I would suggest that you learn to do the same when writing emails to people. In this instance, you should focus on using proper grammar and addressing people in an appropriate manner. On top of this, it would make sense to have a signature that guides people to other presences (e.g., social media, website) that can help them learn more about you. You need to write each email as if you are actually interacting with a person and you are trying to make an impression on them.

Be Fantastic About Follow-Up

One of the lost skill sets of today is the ability to follow-up in an efficient manner when communicating with others. The great news here is you can easily differentiate yourself and your brand from others if you get in the habit of following up on email interactions with others. As a professor, I have found that it is extremely rare for younger generations to consistently follow-up in an efficient manner via email. This is even the case when they are the ones to initiate the contact. The problem here is that individuals do not even realize that poor communication has negative implications for perceptions that other people have about them. If you want to build a unique brand, then pride yourself on being great at following up with others in a timely manner. While you cannot (and should not) feel like you always have to respond immediately, you should certainly get in the habit of responding within a 24-hour time period if it is somebody on whom you are looking to make an impression. Even if they do not fit into this category, keep in mind that the best route is to do this with as many people as possible because you never know when an unexpected connection is going to help you advance your career or your life.

Conduct Messages Like They Are a Press Release

I am certainly not saying you actually have to write messages in the format of a press release here. Or that you need things like quotes to support your key points. Instead, this refers to the fact that the messages you conduct are always public. When you send a message to someone else, you should see it as dialogue that is being released for other people to see. If the topic you are talking about is controversial or if you are being negative about another person, always keep in mind that it is very easy for other people to forward your message and put you in a difficult situation. So, with this in mind, be extremely professional and always write messages that you would be all right being made public.

Under Promise and Over Deliver

Another poor habit that people often form when communicating with others via email is they make promises that they cannot keep. This could certainly be an in-person problem as well, but it is something that definitely comes up when you are communicating with people electronically. Whenever you are discussing a timeline or performance expectation with another person, always get in the habit of under promising and over delivering. In this instance, you should consider the situation and think of a time when you know you can reasonably meet a deadline with a solid product. Once you know this date, set the deadline and then strive to come in early to make an impression on the person. While not everyone will appreciate this, there will certainly be individuals who will see you favorably for being able to follow through. Keep in mind that the deadline must be reasonable to the person in the first place for you to be able to make a positive impression. If you get in the habit of missing deadlines, there is no question you will lose trust with others and this will cost you in credibility.

Put Your Personality Into Messages

Assuming that you have a good personality, it is always good to make sure your messages come across as authentic. If you are a positive person (or are striving to become a positive person), then this is something that should show up in your emails and on social media. If you want people to see you as highly professional, then take the tips in this section and go out of your way to make an impression based on the expectations of the people you are corresponding with. The good news is most people appreciate prompt responses that are written in a clean manner. On top of this, responses are even better when the person has a pleasant personality and you can feel it through the message. Whatever your values are at this point, they should be modeled in your communication via technology when appropriate.

MARKETING MATERIALS

So we have covered some of the areas you should consider when interacting with individuals directly through different technology mediums. Another element you need to consider is the marketing materials you are putting together to make an impression on potential employers and/or partners. We are at a point in which jobs and promotions are extremely competitive and it is necessary for you to learn to always put your best foot forward. One area that is almost always a focal point for people in personal branding is their resume, cover letter, and application materials. One of the challenges here is that people are constantly modeling others (which is good for initial direction), but they rarely take steps to truly differentiate their brand from others'. Your goal should be to put together materials that are so unique and impressive that people are inspired to hire you. Keep in mind that your materials say something about you, and when they are simply average, employers have no reason to think you are anything more than an average candidate.

Make the Most of First Impression

When you think about your marketing materials, consider the fact that many times they are your first impression with a person you are hoping to impress. And many times this will be the only one that you get if you are sending a message that is in line with the status quo. While a differentiated resume created in Adobe InDesign will not guarantee you a job, it sure as heck will make an impression when you embed a video that shows your editing and graphic design skill sets. This is a much better way of modeling these attributes than simply stating them in a traditional resume format. You need to go way beyond just listing your experiences in a plain, uninspiring format. Do something that is so unique that it sends a message about you in the first few seconds of someone picking up your materials. Remind yourself that you often make an intuitive first impression the moment that person comes in to contact with the product you are presenting them. Go big or you might as well go home!

Experience Is More Than Just the Experience

There is no question you need to put experience on your resume if you are entering a field or trying to advance in a field that is highly competitive with an extensive pool of potential candidates. In addition to the actual knowledge you learn and experience that you gain, different experiences provide you with an opportunity to network with individuals who have the potential to help you advance your career. On top of this, your ability alone to pursue and accumulate quality experiences says something about you as a candidate. It shows your passion to advance and an ability to seek out opportunities within your areas of interest. For younger generations, it can tell somebody about the type of person you are because you are willing to go out and gain experience doing things that others are not willing to do. So, when you look at your resume, be sure that it models your passion to realize your vision. When it does, you will have the opportunity to make an impression that will differentiate you from others.

Dare To Be Really Different

Go ahead and start by looking at other people's materials to get an idea of what you can do to enhance your products. If you are able to connect with some creative people, you will likely find collective ideas that will help you start to put together some really solid materials. However, at some point, you need to put these to the side and ask yourself how you can truly make yourself different from your competitors. If you have an ambitious vision, then you will need to learn to expect to be really unique in the way that you approach life. Why not start with the materials you will present to people who can help to advance your career and life? Make it your goal to set an extremely high standard that will push you to put together marketing documents that will open up opportunities. While others are going through the motions to apply for positions, you should be excited about the materials you are sending out because they are something that represents your commitment to excellence.

Take Advantage of User Friendly Technology

For you to be different, there is a good chance you are going to need to be willing to embrace technologies that will force you to step a little out of your comfort zone. We say "a little" here because companies like Adobe and Apple have made it far easier and more cost efficient to develop artistic products that add to our personal brand. While products such as iMovie and InDesign are more user friendly than in the past, there will still be a learning curve and times when you are a little frustrated. However, if being unique matters enough to you, then these are products you can use to make a statement about the type of person that you are. First, you need to make the decision that you are absolutely committed to learning a new skill set. There are no excuses because technology today has provided all the resources you need at your finger tips to learn creative software.

THE ART OF FOLLOWING UP

If you are going to succeed in personal branding and developing relationships, you will need to place a value on networking with people. When you are proactive, there will naturally be opportunities to meet people that can help to advance your career and/or your life. In these instances, you need to be prepared to take steps to connect with these individuals on a personal basis. If there is an individual giving a talk or seminar, stop afterwards to say thank you and be sure to tell them something about the session that you really enjoyed. On top of this, take the time to follow-up (within 2-3 days) to thank them for their time and to let them know how much you appreciate the lessons they shared with you. If you feel comfortable, you can even ask permission to stay in touch with them and explain that you would love the opportunity to talk with them on a personal basis sometime in the near future. When the individual is all right with either one of these things, be great at following up so you are able to develop a solid connection that becomes a part of your network. Another consideration is following up on social media. With the popularity of social media, it makes sense to see if the individual uses sites like Twitter and give a shout out following the session. This is a nice way to initiate conversation even before you follow-up with an email. However, consider whether this would be a good fit for the person you are looking to connect with before you make the post.

THE PERSONAL TOUCH OF A HANDWRITTEN NOTE

With all of the technological advances, it can be easy to get caught up solely relying on email and social media to connect with people. While these are great tools, you should never underestimate the value of a simple handwritten note to show your appreciation. On top of the fact that this shows a nice personal touch, it is important to recognize that there are still a lot of people (especially older generations) that prefer a handwritten note over email dialogue. When you are considering following up with an individual, hopefully you have paid attention to body language and what the person said during the talk so you can make a good decision on whether a handwritten note is the right option. When you decide it is, be sure to follow-up in a timely manner and make sure that the message has a unique personal touch.

Take Home Point—
Take Advantage of Technology

There is no question that face-to-face interaction will always play a major role in your ability to build strong relationships with people who can influence your life. As such, you should invest significant amounts of time making sure you are able to connect with people well. However, technology is a huge part of our society and has serious implications when it comes to building your brand. Social media is not an outlet in which you can go crazy and be something completely different than you are in person. Well, you can, but it will absolutely be a detriment to your reputation because it will lack authenticity. So, make a commitment to making decisions that will add to the strength of your personal brand on a daily basis.

On top of a strategic approach on social media, you can also differentiate yourself from others by making sure you are developing branding materials that will make an impression on the people that see them. For this area, embrace technology and look for ways to have a "WOW" factor that will give you an advantage with individuals you are looking to impress. Take advantage of technology and recognize that the actual presentation of your materials sends a message about what type of person you are before the individual has even read what is in the document. When you get a chance to meet these individuals, be sure you are ready to follow-up in a manner that will continue to give you an edge on competitors. From start to finish, it should always be your goal to make a lasting, extraordinary impression on people that you meet.

IMPRESSIONS IMPLEMENTATION EXERCISE

One of the primary focus areas in the chapter was making sure you are using social media properly to help build your personal brand in an efficient manner. Based on the seven rules presented in the chapter, identify three that will have the biggest impact in your life and commit to making them a part of your social media plan during the next week. As you do this, keep track of how you think this is impacting your personal brand.

CHAPTER 12

Set a Unique Standard of Excellence

~∽~

"Success is the masterful application of the fundamentals on a daily basis."

—Robin Sharma

If you want to make a lasting impression on others, there is a fundamental philosophy you will need to adopt in your life. It is essential that this becomes a central part of your brand as you embark upon a journey to reach your full potential. It is a concept that seems simple in nature, but it is one that is difficult to implement because it requires significant attention and energy to make it happen. As explained by leadership guru Robin Sharma, "Success in life is nothing more than stringing a series of well lived days together like a string of pearls." However, to string these days together, you must commit to setting a unique standard of excellence that will influence others around you. This involves choosing the right values and becoming extraordinary at modeling them every single day as well as you possibly can. In addition to unique self-discipline, this takes a passion to be truly special in all areas of your life. You must set standards that pull you way out of your comfort zone to succeed in developing an extraordinary personal brand. The goal of this chapter will be to help you realize what it will take to become a person who sets a unique standard of excellence in your life.

Don't Let Your Mind Get in the Way

While you are in the process of developing the right habits that are conducive to an extraordinary brand, there will be times when you start to question your ability to achieve your vision. First, understand that this is a natural part of the process and it can take time to develop a mindset that constantly seeks out opportunities. Second, remind yourself that you allowed this doubt to enter your mind and you can just as easily take steps to eliminate it and focus back on growth and realizing your vision. The one thing successful people do extremely well is they learn to block out doubt and instead have faith they will eventually realize their dreams. This should not be confused with an ability to acknowledge weaknesses because this is a part of making sure that you are adjusting and progressing in the right direction. Instead, this relates to times when you allow your mind to get in the way and you question your ability to achieve great things. This is when you need to step in and remind yourself of the reason why you are pursuing your vision. If you have chosen something that is strong enough, your mind will get back on track and focus on growth towards the end goal.

It is also important to comprehend that you will never realize your full potential if you do not learn to dream big. Many times you will unconsciously place limitations on what you can achieve and you must learn to eliminate this terrible habit. Work hard to develop your mind to believe you can achieve great things. Wake up each morning and tell yourself you have everything within your power to realize your vision. When you learn to make your mind an advocate, there are very few limitations to the things in life that you can achieve. And with the right framework, you can develop a personal brand that will allow you to achieve amazing things with people.

BE WILLING TO STEP WAY OUT OF YOUR COMFORT ZONE

The only way you can set an extraordinary standard of excellence is by stepping way out of your comfort zone. When you choose a vision that is lofty enough, there will be no choice but to constantly get out of your comfort zone to move towards full potential. This is exactly the type of process you need to embrace. If you want to achieve unique things in your life, then you need to seek out opportunities that will provide you with the greatest opportunities to grow. I believe you will quickly find it is the situations that make us the most uncomfortable that give us the best opportunity to stretch ourselves and to move towards full potential. When you move towards situations that challenge you, there is no question you are going to increase your rate of failure. However, this is not a bad thing because the process of challenging ourselves and falling short is a part of being successful. Thus, if you want to realize your brand vision, you need to learn to embrace a mindset in which you are not afraid of failing.

EMBRACE FAILURE AS A NORMAL PART OF THE PROCESS

When you pay attention to the people around you, it will quickly become apparent that most people are scared to death of failing. In many instances, they are simply afraid of what they will look like if they fall short of their pursuit to achieve something. This is silly when you think about it. Does it really matter if we fall short and someone criticizes us? If you have set a lofty goal, pursued it with a passion, and fallen short, there is absolutely nothing you need to be ashamed of. In fact, you should be proud of your efforts because you gave it your best and were willing to step out of your comfort zone. And while you did not realize your goal, you can be sure that you will absolutely grow from the experience if you have the right mindset and learn from your mistakes. It is this process that will eventually catapult you to achieve great things in your life. If you don't believe me, check out this quote from Michael Jordan, one of the greatest athletes of all time: "I've missed more than 9000 shots in my career. I've lost almost 300 games. 26 times, I've been trusted to take the game winning shot and missed. I've failed over and over and over again in my life. And that is why I succeed."

You can be sure that Michael Jordan did not internalize failure when he missed all those shots and lost all of those games. Instead, he simply saw it as part of the process necessary to achieve his goals. For many people, they take the opposite route of Michael Jordan and tend to internalize failures when they fall short of their goals. Because of this, they see themselves as failures instead of seeing the situation as a temporary setback. With this mindset, you can see why these individuals would simply avoid situations that present any chances of failing. However, the problem is you cannot succeed when you stay in a place that is comfortable. When you are setting lofty expectations for yourself, it is inevitable that you will fall short on a regular basis during the process. Through these failures, you have an opportunity to learn and move forward with valuable insights. Despite the fact that you fell short of your expectations, the process will likely move you much closer to your vision than if you simply sat back and did not challenge yourself. This is exactly the reason why you need to develop a mindset where you see failure as a normal part of the process. While you should never seek out failure simply to fall short, it is important that you challenge yourself in a way which you will fall short from time to time. And when this happens, do not take it too personally. Instead, take the time to reflect on why you failed and learn from your experience. When you do this often enough, you will eventually learn to overcome certain situations and you will be far more efficient.

SET "STRETCH GOALS" TO ENCOURAGE GROWTH

When you are attempting to realize an extraordinary personal brand, you will need to learn to set "stretch goals" that pull you way out of your comfort zone. If you have not heard of stretch goals, they are extremely ambitious goals that require you to consider the way you are doing things because your current skill sets and approach are not up to par for the challenge. At the moment, you can see these as dream goals because they are likely not currently something you can achieve in the immediate future. Please know that you will never have the ability to comprehend this process if you are not able to get comfortable with the idea of embracing failure. In addition to embracing this process, you will need to develop a proactive mindset in which you have an expectation that you are going to just figure out how to make things happen. It doesn't matter if you don't know how to make it happen right now because you are going to figure it out on the move.

When you are considering stretch goals, understand that there are different time ranges for these expectations. At the moment, if you are an undergraduate student, you might have a dream to one day become an Athletic Director at a major Division I institution. First off, good for you for taking the time to know what your dream is in your professional career. While this may change as you evolve as a person, this stretch goal by itself will get you moving to improve your skill sets. As you consider how to make this dream happen, it is logical that you would map out a career progression that considers some of the necessary steps in the process. In the short-term, it would make sense to have a stretch goal to become a part of one of the top graduate programs in sport administration in the United States (e.g., University of North Carolina Sport Administration) because of the fact that athletic departments place a value on advanced education. However, as you research the criteria for admission, you quickly realize the admissions process is intense and you need to develop a better resume with more experience to make yourself competitive. Thus, another immediate checkpoint might be finding a solid internship in a Division I athletic department so you can gain experience, develop skill sets, and create connections to take your next step. To obtain this internship, you may need to step way out of your comfort zone while reaching out to complete strangers in order to increase your chances of getting the position. The point is you will have a variety of situations like this you will need to pursue if you are going to reach your dream of becoming an Athletic Director. As we have discussed in this chapter, there will be times when you will fail at achieving your stretch goals. Rather than internalize these short falls, be like Michael Jordan and learn from your failure so you can stay on track to realizing your dream. It is so important you continue to set expectations for yourself that force you in to situations that stretch you as a person and as a professional. If you do this enough, you will eventually become a completely different person with a tolerance for much higher challenges without even realizing it.

SUCCESS IS NOT A STRAIGHT PATH

When you set out on your pursuit to realize your brand vision, it is important that you understand that there will be setbacks on the road to success. You already know this because we have developed a mindset in which we will challenge ourselves so much that failure will be inevitable. With this in mind, it is natural that our progression to realizing full potential will not be a straight line. While many people think that this will be the case, it doesn't take you long studying successful people to know they have had more than their share of failures. Take Abraham Lincoln for example (who we studied earlier in this book), his road to becoming the President of the United States and emancipating slaves was nothing remotely close to being a straight path to success. His failures were extensive and were no doubt a part of him eventually becoming the great leader that inspired positive change and left a legacy for the world. Your path to building a unique brand that leaves a legacy will be no different. However, you can make this process much more efficient if you develop the ability to quickly learn from your mistakes and make consistent growth a part of your personal brand.

DO IT EVEN WHEN IT DOESN'T SEEM TO MATTER

Allow me to let you in on a little secret about branding. Anybody can build a solid brand when things are going well and it is easy to make the right decisions. However, life will not always provide you with the ideal conditions to make sound decisions. In fact, in most instances, it will be difficult to make the right types of investments on a daily basis if we do not have the right structure in place. The process of differentiation, making yourself unique in comparison to others, is directly influenced by your ability to do the little things even when there are no tangible benefits for doing so. If your vision matters to you enough, you need to make the decision that you will follow through on your intentions on a regular basis. The good news here is that if you do this enough, eventually it will become more like a habit and will feel far more natural. In the meantime, take Nike's advice and make the decision to "just do it" when it comes to the things that matter most to you!

DON'T SELL YOURSELF SHORT

As humans, we sometimes sell ourselves way short of the things that we can accomplish in life. In fact, I would say that 99% of all people have no real idea of what they are capable of if they were able to get their mind right and if they pursued their vision with a passion. Don't be a part of the group of people who settles for less than their full potential. If you have done this in the past, then make the decision today that you will no longer do this to yourself. Strive to commit fully to understanding what your vision is and then pursue it with your full attention and energy every single day. As you consider this decision, think about this quote on regret by leadership guru Robin Sharma: "At the end of your life, it'll be the risks that you didn't take versus the ones you did that most fill you with regret." Make a decision to avoid this situation and strive for full potential every day moving forward!

TAKE HOME POINT— SET A UNIQUE STANDARD OF EXCELLENCE

At this point in the book, my hope is you have an initial vision in your mind that gets you excited when you think about it. After this chapter, it is smart to consider whether you feel your vision is lofty enough that it will challenge you to change drastically as a person. If it does not, then at least consider the fact that you may be selling yourself short, and that it might be worthwhile to stop and think of something more suitable to your passion, talent level, and work ethic. When you think about this vision, it is likely you will not be exactly sure how you will realize this "stretch goal" in the future. This is where you need to pursue your vision with a belief that you will chase it down through a string of lessons learned from challenging yourself. There will be failures in the process that will leave you questioning your ability to achieve the vision, but you need to constantly remind yourself that you will prevail if you stick to the values you set for yourself earlier in this book. And if this does not work, use Abraham Lincoln and Michael Jordan as inspirations when you feel like giving in to failure. You never know when your dream will be waiting just beyond one of the failures you are facing.

IMPRESSIONS IMPLEMENTATION EXERCISE

If you are going to realize full potential, you need to embrace failure as a part of the process. As you plan for your upcoming week, consider the opportunities in which you can stretch yourself in key value areas. Once you have brainstormed these elements, commit to following through on three of the areas throughout the week.

CHAPTER 13

Above and Beyond Mentality:
10 Commandments for Building
a Powerful Personal Brand

⚬⚬⚬

"I am always doing that which I cannot do, in order to learn how to do it."

—*Pablo Picasso*

We are at the point in this book in which you should have a good feel for personal branding and how you can take steps to increase your chances of success in the future. My hope is you are excited to get out and make your vision a reality through hard work and a constant willingness to step out of your comfort zone. If this is the way you are feeling, then we will cap things off with 10 more tips that will help you take your personal branding efforts to an entirely new level. Because you are committed to cultivating an extraordinary reputation, you can see these as branding commandments to embrace on a daily basis. By developing the ability to do these things consistently, you can feel confident you are well on your way to making some memorable impressions on the people around you. Let's just jump right into things and touch on the 10 Personal Branding Commandments.

Commandment #1:
Aspire To Be AWESOME in All That You Do

Nobody really gets involved in personal branding to be average. You sure as heck have not read this much of the book in hopes of going out and settling for the status quo. If you are going to spend time striving to build your brand, then you might as well just make plans right now to be extraordinary. The best way to ensure this occurs is to strive to be AWESOME in all areas of your life. When you fully grasp the concepts in this book, you will start to realize that you have the ability to control all of the interactions you have with people in your life. With this realization, you can go out and make sure that they are nothing short of outstanding. While you will make some mistakes from time to time, there is no reason why you should ever lose sight of wanting to live an extraordinary life.

Commandment #2:
Take an Active Interest in Testimonials

When leadership expert Jim Rohn discusses the pursuit of success, he mentions the importance of getting people who will speak on your behalf. He calls these testimonials and explains that they are achieved when you are able to make a positive impression on people.[1] In the marketing world, these are called word-of-mouth promotions and they are exactly what you need to achieve if you are going to develop an extraordinary personal brand. When you have interactions with people, your goal should be for them to be so strong that people will be inclined to tell others about you. When this occurs, Mr. Rohn explains that success will more naturally come to you because you will have learned how to add value to people. Walt Disney illustrated this best when he said, "What ever you do, do it well. Do it so well that when people see you do it they will want to come back and see you do it again and they will want to bring others and show them how well you do what you do."

Commandment #3:
Develop an Ability to Add Serious Value

When you think about building an extraordinary brand, one of the things you absolutely must be able to do is add tremendous value to the people around you. Think about it. All of the amazing people and organizations we have talked about from a branding and leadership perspective all have one thing in common: at the center of their approach is an ability to add unique value to their customers or followers. So, if you want to build a reputation that people will remember, and eventually talk about, you need to make it a top priority to learn to add value to people. Roger Goodell, the commissioner of the National Football League (NFL), is seen as highly influential in the sport industry. In fact, recently Sports Illustrated named him as the "most powerful person in sports" in a list that included ESPN President John Skipper, IOC President Jacques Rogge and Nike Chairman Phil Knight.[2] The impressive thing about Commissioner Goodell is that he started at the bottom of the league and worked his way up by developing a reputation as an individual who was constantly able to tackle tough tasks. In an informal question and answer session with Goodell, the topic of advancing was asked and he responded by saying the following:

> "You have to deliver value. You can be the smartest person in the room, and if you cannot work with people and you do not see the big objective, you are not going to succeed. I never once asked for a promotion, I never once asked for a raise in my entire career. My theory was to go and find areas where I can contribute things that I thought would be big challenges for the NFL. If you do that, you are going to continue to develop as an individual."[3]

The point here is branding has a lot to do with developing the ability to add value to the people around you. If you are able to contribute to key individuals in your career and your life, then you will advance and experience success.

Commandment #4:
Learn To Be a Likable Person

There are all kinds of personalities in the world and I would never tell you that you need to be something that you are not. Even if I did, this would not work because your approach has to be authentic to the type of person you are or you will eventually fail in building relationships with others. However, if you embrace the concept of adding value and combine that with treating people well, there is a good chance that you can become a more likable person. It is important to remember to be humble and to approach relationships with the right motives in mind. When you become a likable person, there is a stronger likelihood that people will want to be around you and contribute to your vision.

Commandment #5:
Do Your Best to Be Kind, But Not to Please Everyone

There is a part of branding that has to do with respecting people and learning to treat them the right way. The Golden Rule should always apply when attempting to build a personal brand that cultivates extraordinary relationships. However, it is important to understand that there is a fine line here when it comes to being kind and trying to please everyone. Your job is to learn to live your values the best way possible and feel 100 percent confident you are living in a manner that aligns with the person you want to become. As you progress, there is a strong likelihood you will have people that will question you even when you are living extremely well. As explained by philosopher Ralph Waldo Emerson, "Whatever course you decide upon, there will always be someone to tell you that you are wrong." This is particularly true if you are in some form of leadership and you start to realize success. You need to remind yourself that it is not your job to please everyone. You should certainly do your best to make a strategic impression on key individuals, but the most important element in personal branding is becoming great at modeling your values on a consistent basis. If you model in an extraordinary manner and people don't like it, you can live with that.

Commandment #6:
Thrive at the Concept of "Thin Splicing"

In *Blink: The Power of Thinking Without Thinking*, author Malcolm Gladwell presents the concept of "thin splicing" when it comes to realizing success in life.[4] In essence, this relates to an individual's ability to make instant sound decisions based on their experiences in life. While there are a variety of factors that go into this process, this is absolutely something that can be influenced by the investment you make in strategic growth initiatives. For example, when you regularly read books on communicating with people effectively and are constantly evaluating your performance, your mind will process this information and you will increase your chances of making sound decisions. The outstanding news here is that strategic repetition can pay big dividends because your brain will learn from the process and evolve. So, with this in mind, embrace initiatives on a daily basis that will develop your skill sets in key areas. As you question whether to follow through on these initiatives, remind yourself that this is exactly what it takes for you to realize full potential. Do the little things consistently, and eventually big things will happen. It's worth the investment to thrive in your "thin splicing" ability.

Commandment #7:
Never Underestimate the Value of an Individual Action

If there is one thing you should have learned in this book by now, it is likely that your actions matter when it comes to branding, relationships, and success. Every single one of them! When you pay attention to the people who have made a lasting impression on you, it is likely you will find that these individuals are great at living in the moment and making each interaction with people count. If you want to follow in their path to success, you need to follow the same formula. Make it your goal to be great in every single interaction you have on a daily basis. Do not neglect the ones that come with people you perceive as being unimportant because every one accumulates when it comes to personal branding. Remind yourself it is one of these individuals who will eventually be in a role to help enhance your life at some point. Even if this were not the case, this is absolutely the right thing to do and this will result in testimonials that will enhance your life.

Commandment #8:
Make Each Day a Masterpiece

In his book *Make Today Count*, Dr. John Maxwell discusses the importance of striving to make each day a masterpiece.[5] To do this, there is no question that you must have a mentality in which you are waking up focused on being great at modeling your values. In personal branding, this is how you cultivate extraordinary relationships and make a lasting impression on people who have the ability to add value to your life. You take control of each day and try to make it the best that you possibly can. From start to finish, it should be your goal to live every single day to the fullest so you never have regrets. As you develop the ability to string together these extremely well-lived days, you will be well on your way to realizing your full potential and making an impact on the people around you. It all starts with a simple philosophy that has the capability to have a profound impact on your life.

Commandment #9:
Make Reflecting and Evolving a Part of Your Repertoire

If you are going to live each day to the fullest, there will be certain steps you must take to make sure you are constantly building on your efforts. As you move through your days, it is likely you will have ones that will go great and this will provide you with momentum to push forward towards your vision. On the flip side, there will also be ones that are extremely difficult that will cause you to question your ability to achieve great things. In both of these instances, it is important that you take the time to reflect on your efforts at the end of each day. It is often best to do this in a journal so that you are able to document your process. When you have good days, you can write about what worked for you and how you can improve on your efforts to ensure you have more days exactly like this and even better. For the bad days, you have the opportunity to explore the reasons why you fell short of expectations and how to avoid them in the future. In addition, you can take a proactive approach here to make sure you are ending each entry by focusing on the positive. This step alone makes it worthwhile because it will teach you to find the positive in challenging situations. Once you have taken this all into account, it is critical to consider the ways you can evolve to make sure you are moving in the right direction to realize your vision. Constant growth is the one way to make certain you are living a life that will allow you to reach your full potential.

Commandment #10:
Just Learn To Be Yourself

One of the best tips you can possibly receive in personal branding is to just learn to be yourself. If you are thinking that you are not happy with what you currently are, then commit to becoming something much better through the process we have described in this book. The one way to maximize your chances of success and happiness in your life is by setting extremely high standards and then following through on them on a regular basis. When you are living your values, it is extremely easy to be yourself because your actions and words will be in alignment, and you will not feel like you have anything to hide. When this occurs, you will come across as real and there will be an authentic feel to your approach. Whether people agree with your values or not, they can usually appreciate someone who is real and is living the things that they believe in. You will be amazed how satisfying it is when you are living the way you know you should be living. The confidence that comes with this alone is something that will pay big dividends in your pursuit.

ADDED-VALUE TIP:
MAKE SURE YOUR GLASS IS ALWAYS HALF FULL

If you are at this point in the book, you are serious about making decisions to improve your life and to build a brand that makes an extraordinary impression on others. I applaud you for committing to make this decision because it is a noble pursuit that will change your life if you are persistent with your efforts. However, there is an element that we have not covered in-depth specifically in this book that is critical for success in branding. If you want to reach full potential in your relationships, then you need to become a person who is positive and who people want to be around. When you develop the ability to always see the glass as half full, you will focus on the positive and will naturally be more productive throughout your entire day. On the flip side, people who are negative tend to focus more on negative things that slow up their entire day. Life coach extraordinaire Anthony Robbins explains in his "The Edge" album that you will get more of the things that you focus on in your life.[6] So, if you make the choice to always see things as at least half full, you will be far more likely to attract good results in your life.

TAKE HOME POINT—
GO ABOVE AND BEYOND EXPECTATIONS!

The goal of this chapter was to give you tangible tips to focus on as you embark on your journey to build an extraordinary personal brand and life. With the right foundation in place from the earlier chapters, you can now focus on implementing these tips one day at a time until they are a part of your daily approach. Once you get to this point, it is far easier to develop a personal brand that is authentic and positioned in a way that will be better received by the people around you. However, even when this is the case, you still need to make sure you are diligent about doing the little things on a daily basis. As you wake up each morning, you should get out of bed looking to make each day a masterpiece by striving to make awesome impressions on the people around you. If you are able to do this effectively with each of the commandments, there is no doubt that you will get to the point where you are receiving amazing testimonials. It is all about the fundamentals in branding and you are about ready to head off on your journey to live the best life that you possibly can!

IMPRESSIONS IMPLEMENTATION EXERCISE

In the chapter, we discussed the importance of earning quality testimonials from the people that surround us in the pursuit to build an extraordinary personal brand. Building on our previous target market exercise, write down the testimonials that you would like to receive from these individuals in the future. In addition, take notes on the specific tips covered in this chapter that will be critical to realizing these testimonials. Once you are done, put this in a place where you can see it on a daily basis.

CHAPTER 14

You Have Everything You Need to Build an Extraordinary Brand . . . Now Make it Happen!!!

"Nobody ever said it would be easy, they just promised it would be worth it."

—Harvey MacKay

I f you have made it to this point in the book, then you deserve a pat on the back. If you have read the entire book and applied all of the concepts, then you deserve a congratulations because very few people actually commit to following through on intentions. In fact, research has shown that only 43% of the people who start a book actually read the entire thing.[1] It is safe to assume that applying the concepts in this book consistently over time would apply to an even fewer amount of people because it represents a larger investment. I feel confident that you will be in the small minority that takes steps and changes your life drastically moving forward!

The good news for you is that everyone has the ability to take control of their brand and make it something truly special. There are a few things you need to understand though. First, be aware that personal branding is an ongoing, time-intensive process because people generally have to learn about you before they are comfortable making an assessment. While branding is an intuitive process, there is a level of comfort that people need to have before they are willing to speak on your behalf. Second, understand that this process will take even longer if you have neglected your brand in the past and have developed poor relationships with people. There is no question that it takes much longer to rebuild a brand that has been tarnished than it does to build one from a fresh start. Third, understand that you should absolutely take the time to comprehend exactly who you want to be if you hope to maximize your efforts in personal branding. Finally, if you are willing to make the investment, know that it will be worth it because there are some amazing benefits that come from building an extraordinary reputation.

It's Worth the Investment

There are so many benefits that come with making a sound investment to build an extraordinary brand. Strengthened personal relationships, advanced professional career, and/or newly cultivated business opportunities are a few of the benefits that are realized from modeling the right values on a daily basis. When you consider key individuals in your life, determine values that are important to them, and then model them on a daily basis, you put yourself in a position to be a person of authentic influence. In essence, by learning to add real value to the people around you on a regular basis, you are cultivating a brand that will open up opportunities in your life. It's like the lesson we learned from the legendary influencer Zig Ziglar that you can achieve anything in life if you help enough people to achieve their dreams. This is a recipe for success you can make happen by striving to achieve a lofty brand vision that puts people first.

THE "HEAD FAKE"

In Randy Pausch's *The Last Lecture*, he discusses the life lessons that can make your life great in front of a room full of people. At the end, he admits that there is a "head fake" that took place during the entire talk because the audience thinks the speech was for them. In fact, the entire thing was dedicated to his family who attended this final talk.[2] If you have not guessed it already, this book has a "head fake" that you may not have seen coming. While personal branding is an extremely important concept, what this book is really about is learning to live an extraordinary life. It is about far more than just seeking personal gain. While it is certainly all right to see value in advancing your career and life, this cannot come at the sacrifice of taking advantage of the people around you. The real meaningful results come when you develop a selfless philosophy in which you learn to put other people first on a day-to-day basis. While this sounds fairly straight forward, it is actually extremely difficult and is something that I personally struggle with on a daily basis as I try to keep my ego in check. While it can be a tough adjustment, it is worth sacrificing for, because adding value to others in a selfless manner is an attribute you want associated with your brand. It will eventually build loyalty with people, and with loyalty comes real lasting contributions—both from others and eventually to you.

DON'T EXPECT EASY

If you always expect things to come easy, I would suggest that you get used to being disappointed because life is not an easy process. As we covered when discussing the legendary leaders Abraham Lincoln, Martin Luther King Jr., Walt Disney, and Steve Jobs, all meaningful contributions (and the associated legacy) come from individuals who have a passionate vision and a willingness to sacrifice as they chase it down daily. They were able to achieve great things because they did not expect the process to be easy. Instead, they stayed focused on their vision and demonstrated a self-discipline daily to live in a manner that would eventually allow them to realize their dreams. Similar to these individuals, you need to develop the ability to fight off the urge to get complacent when contemplating whether you should follow through on your intentions. When you expect things to be difficult and you cultivate an efficiency in following through, you will be well on your way to achieving unique things in your life.

NOW GO BE GREAT!!!

As we come to the end of the book, I would like to point out that there is nothing stopping you from cultivating an extraordinary brand. If you commit to living the concepts we covered in this book, you will enhance the relationships in your life and new opportunities will present themselves that you may have previously not considered possible. However, you need to commit to the fundamentals over time before you will realize the compounding nature of branding. If you demonstrate discipline in your pursuit to build an extraordinary brand, your life will be more fulfilling than you ever thought possible. It is for this reason that you should pursue greatness when it comes to living the right way! You have far too many gifts to ever settle for anything less than great!

CLOSING THOUGHTS

I would like to thank you for giving your time to learn about the steps you can take to change your life. While I don't know you personally, I truly believe you have everything necessary to build an extraordinary brand if you are still reading and learning with me. Be confident in your ability to live so well that realizing your vision is only a matter of time. And as you pursue your passions with all of your energy each day, be sure that you are taking the time to smile and enjoy all of life's gifts. After all, none of this matters too much if you are not enjoying the process. With that being said, it is now time to go out and make your own dent in the universe! Be like Lincoln and leave a legacy that people will talk about long after you are gone!

NOTES

3. Vision Is a Vital Starting Point in Branding

1. Oates, S. B. (1994). With malice toward none: A life of Abraham Lincoln. HarperCollins Publishing: New York, NY.

2. Abraham Lincoln (ND). Retrieved from: http://www.biography.com/people/abraham-lincoln-9382540.

3. About Dr. King (ND). Retrieved from: http://www.thekingcenter.org/about-dr-king.

4. Walt Disney (ND). Retrieved from: http://www.biography.com/people/walt-disney-9275533#awesm=~oCnqT76wNs8R9O.

5. Isaacson, W. (2011). *Steve Jobs*. Simon & Schuster Paperbacks: New York, NY.

5. Become a Master at Modeling Values

1. Gandhi, M. (1993). *The Story of My Experiments With Truth*. Beacon Press: Boston, MA.

6. The Importance of Specificity in Branding

1. http://sethgodin.typepad.com/seths_blog/2009/12/define-brand.html

2. Isaacson, W. (2011). Steve Jobs. Simon & Schuster Paperbacks: New York, NY.

3. The World's Most Valuable Brands. (2013). Retrieved from: http://www.forbes.com/powerful-brands/list/.

7. Aspire for Authenticity in Daily Interactions

1. Managing Your 50,000 Daily Thoughts. (2007). *Scientific Developments*. Retrieved from: http://www.sentientdevelopments.com/2007/03/managing-your-50000-daily-thoughts.html.

9. Cultivate a Care Mindset for People

1. Maxwell, J. (ND). *Establishing Credibility*. Retrieved from: https://www.johnmaxwell.com/store/products/Establishing-Credibility-%5BDigital%252dMP3%5D.html.

2. Hsieh, T. (2010). *Delivering Happiness: A Path to Profits, Passion, and Purpose*. Business Plus: New York, NY.

3. Gallo, C. (2013). *How Southwest and Virgin America Win By Putting People Before Profit*. Retrieved from: http://www.forbes.com/sites/carminegallo/2013/09/10/how-southwest-and-virgin-america-win-by-putting-people-before-profit/.

4. Rapping Flight Attendant from Southwest Airlines. (2009). Retrieved from: https://www.youtube.com/watch?v=G9lZV_828OA.

10. Insist on Being Extraordinary at Individual Interactions

1. The Journey. (2014). *The Official Site of John Wooden*. Retrieved from: http://www.coachwooden.com/index2.html.

11. Capitalizing on Key Brand Interaction Spots

1. The 15 Most Popular Social Networking Sites. (2014). *eBiz: The Business*. Retrieved from: http://www.ebizmba.com/articles/social-networking-websites.

13. Ten Tips to Building Powerful Personal Brand

1. Rohn, J. (2005). Success Equations/Personal Development. Downloaded from iTunes.

2. SI's 50 Most Powerful People in Sports (2012). Retrieved from:

http://sportsillustrated.cnn.com/main/photos/1303/50-most-powerful-people-in-sports/9/.

3. Roger Goodell on Internships and Adding value (2013). Retrieved from: https://www.youtube.com/watch?v=BRl_s62sMyY.

4. Gladwell, M. (2005). *Blink: The Power of Thinking Without Thinking.* Little, Brown and Company: New York, NY.

5. Maxwell, J. (2004). *Make Today Count: The Secret of Your Success is Determined* By Your Daily Agenda. Center Street: New York, NY.

6. Robbins, A. (2006). *The Edge: The Power to Change Your Life Today.* Downloaded from iTunes.

14. You Have Everything You Need To Build an Extraordinary Brand . . . Now Make it Happen!!!

1. Reading statistics. (2014). Retrieved from: http://www.statisticbrain.com/reading-statistics/.

2. Randy Pausch Last Lecture: Achieving Your Childhood Dreams. (2007). Retrieved from: https://www.youtube.com/watch?v=ji5_MqicxSo.

ABOUT THE AUTHOR

D r. Coyte Cooper is currently an Assistant Professor and Graduate Coordinator in Sport Administration at the University of North Carolina (UNC) at Chapel Hill where he teaches Sport Marketing courses at both the graduate and undergraduate levels. With a research line focused on "Innovative Branding Strategies in College Sport Environments," he has published 38 peer-reviewed articles, 8 book chapters, and the *Marketing Manual*. Dr. Cooper is also the founder and CEO of Elite Level Sport Marketing (ELSM), which is a firm that focuses on providing branding training to sport organizations, programs, and leaders. He earned his Doctorate in Sport Marketing & Management from Indiana University—Bloomington in 2007. He currently resides in Durham, North Carolina with his wife Brandy and his two kids Carter and Mya.

Corporate Presentations

⌘

If you are interested in having Dr. Cooper talk to your group about "Impressions" and developing a mindset conducive to productivity and living an extraordinary life, please use the contact information below to get more information. Dr. Cooper will create custom presentations that are tailored to your unique environment and/or situation. He'll explain how the concept of personal branding can be used to maximize chances of success (and happiness) for both individuals and organizations.

Capitalize on "Impressions" in Unique Settings (Examples)

➤ Fortune 500 companies

➤ Professional sport organizations

➤ College/high school athletic departments

➤ University classrooms

Contact Dr. Cooper

To book Dr. Cooper for your event or for more information on "Impressions" presentations, visit www.coytecooper.com.

⌘

"The Impressions (and personal branding) concept has the potential to transform any group interested in developing highly focused and purposeful individuals"

Resources to Help You Make a Unique Impression

⁓⁓⁓

Now that you have finished reading *Impressions: The Power of Personal Branding in Living an Extraordinary Life,* you have taken the first steps towards maximizing full potential. To help reinforce the messages, we have created some additional resources to guide you in the future. Below are a few of the resources we have created to help you make positive impressions on the people around you.

One-of-a-Kind Content at www.coytecooper.com

➢ Impressions blog with application entries relating to book.

➢ Monthly "Quick Impressions Podcast" with tips on how to leave lasting impressions on a regular basis.

➢ Ask the author section for questions on making extraordinary impressions with others.

Follow Author on Social Media

Follow Coyte on Twitter: https://twitter.com/coytecooper

Follow Coyte on Instagram: http://instagram.com/coytecooper

AUTHOR IMPRESSIONS

⚰

"The UNC Graduate Sport Administration Program could not be in better hands than it is with Dr. Coyte Cooper at the helm. As one of his former students in Chapel Hill, I had the privilege of being prepared for a career in college athletics through his enthusiastic, passionate and inspiring approach. He teaches through the lens of a former student-athlete who always has his students best interests in mind and always brings his savvy marketing approach to the table. I'll be the first in line to buy his book so he can continue to help me learn and grow, just as he has when I was his student."

—Jordan Skolnick, Director of Development
(University of Michigan)

"From my first day of having Dr. Cooper as a professor, it was easy to see the passion that he had in the professional and personal growth of his students. He came in every day with high energy and always stressed the importance of going above and beyond in every aspect of our lives. More importantly, Dr. Cooper has been a significant mentor in my life and has helped me develop greatly as a young professional and as a person."

—Joe Smaldone, Current Sport Administration Graduate Student
(University of North Carolina - Chapel Hill)

"Dr. Coyte Cooper's contributions to the sport of wrestling have been immeasurable. He has been extraordinarily effective at helping college and high school wrestling coaches enhance the brand of their wrestling programs by emphasizing the right values and teaching programs how to communicate with key stakeholders."

—Mike Moyer, Executive Director
(National Wrestling Coaches Association)

"I have always believed in branding from an organizational standpoint, but Coyte has led me to think about branding from a different perspective. The personal impressions you leave on people ultimately define who you are and has the unique potential for impacting people's lives. In my role as a university professor and administrator, not to mention my life as a husband and father of four children, I have the opportunity to be a game changer. This book has caused me to think deeply about my personal connections with those whom I interact, and how the impressions I make on them can lead to positive outcomes. If you know Coyte Cooper, or anything about him, you will want to read Impressions."

—Kevin Guskiewicz, Ph.D., Kenan
Distinguished Professor, Senior Associate Dean in College of Arts and Sciences
(University of North Carolina)

"Our Athletics Department had the privilege to host Dr. Cooper to train our coaching staff on branding. His delivery, content, and passion made a lasting impression on our staff. He has been an unbelievable resource and probably the best professional development I have been able to provide during my tenure, because building programs also takes place off the fields."

—Bob Hartman, Athletic Director
(Whitehall High School)

CPSIA information can be obtained at www.ICGtesting.com
Printed in the USA
BVOW08s2342221115

428084BV00002B/43/P